The Science Behind Demand Forecasting A Layman's Perspective

Bentley Finn

Copyright © [2023]

Title: The Science Behind Demand Forecasting A Layman's Perspective
Author's: Bentley Finn

This book was printed and published by [Publisher's: **Bentley Finn**] in [2023]

ISBN:

TABLE OF CONTENT

Chapter 3: Demand Forecasting Techniques 32

Moving Averages

Weighted Moving Averages

Exponential Smoothing

Regression Analysis

Time Series Analysis

Causal Models

Chapter 4: Data Collection and Analysis 44

Data Sources for Demand Forecasting

Internal Data Sources

External Data Sources

Data Cleaning and Preprocessing

Statistical Analysis Techniques

Descriptive Statistics

Correlation Analysis

Hypothesis Testing

Chapter 1: Introduction to Demand Forecasting

What is Demand Forecasting?

Demand forecasting is a critical aspect of operations and supply chain management that helps businesses predict the future demand for their products or services. It involves using historical data, statistical models, and market research to estimate the quantity of goods or services that customers will require in the future. By accurately forecasting demand, companies can make informed decisions regarding production, inventory management, and resource allocation.

In the fast-paced and ever-changing business environment we live in today, demand forecasting has become an essential tool for businesses of all sizes. It allows companies to streamline their operations, optimize their supply chains, and ultimately increase their profitability. By understanding customer demand patterns, businesses can improve their efficiency, reduce costs, and enhance customer satisfaction.

Demand forecasting can be done at various levels, ranging from short-term to long-term forecasts. Short-term forecasts typically cover a period of up to three months and are crucial for day-to-day operational planning, such as inventory management and production scheduling. On the other hand, long-term forecasts span over a year or more and are used for strategic decision-making, such as capacity planning and market expansion.

There are several methods and techniques used in demand forecasting, including qualitative and quantitative approaches. Qualitative methods rely on expert opinions, market surveys, and consumer feedback to predict demand. These methods are useful when historical data is scarce or when introducing new products into the market. Quantitative methods, on the other hand, utilize mathematical and statistical models to analyze historical data and project future demand. These models include time series analysis, regression analysis, and machine learning algorithms.

While demand forecasting is not an exact science, it provides valuable insights that help businesses make informed decisions. It enables companies to align their production capacity with customer demand, avoid stockouts or excess inventory, and plan their resources effectively. By accurately forecasting demand, businesses can improve their operational efficiency, reduce costs, and gain a competitive edge in the market.

In conclusion, demand forecasting is a vital component of operations and supply chain management. It helps businesses anticipate customer demand, optimize their resources, and make informed decisions. By understanding the science behind demand forecasting, companies can enhance their efficiency, improve customer satisfaction, and achieve long-term success.

Importance of Demand Forecasting

Subchapter: Importance of Demand Forecasting

In the ever-evolving landscape of business, one aspect that remains constant is the importance of demand forecasting. Whether you are a small business owner or a supply chain manager in a multinational corporation, understanding and accurately predicting consumer demand is crucial for success. This subchapter delves into the significance of demand forecasting and its relevance in the field of operations and supply chain management.

Demand forecasting is the process of estimating the future demand for a product or service. It involves analyzing historical data, market trends, and various factors that can impact demand, such as economic conditions, consumer behavior, and technological advancements. By harnessing the power of data and analytical techniques, businesses can make informed decisions and optimize their operations.

One of the primary benefits of demand forecasting is its ability to reduce uncertainty. By accurately predicting future demand, businesses can align their production, inventory management, and supply chain activities accordingly. This ensures that products are available when and where customers need them, minimizing stockouts and overstock situations. Consequently, demand forecasting helps companies optimize their inventory levels, reduce carrying costs, and improve overall operational efficiency.

Moreover, demand forecasting plays a pivotal role in new product development and marketing strategies. By understanding customer preferences and anticipating market trends, businesses can develop innovative products and tailor their marketing campaigns effectively.

This not only enhances customer satisfaction but also helps companies stay ahead of their competitors.

For supply chain management professionals, demand forecasting provides valuable insights into capacity planning and resource allocation. By accurately predicting demand, businesses can adjust their production schedules, manage their workforce, and source raw materials accordingly. This enables organizations to optimize their supply chain operations, reduce lead times, and enhance customer service levels.

Demand forecasting also facilitates collaborative decision-making and effective communication among various stakeholders. By sharing accurate forecasts with suppliers, retailers, and other partners, businesses can align their activities, reduce supply chain disruptions, and improve overall coordination. This collaborative approach fosters trust and strengthens relationships, leading to mutual benefits for all parties involved.

In conclusion, demand forecasting is an essential tool for businesses in the field of operations and supply chain management. It enables organizations to reduce uncertainty, optimize inventory levels, enhance customer satisfaction, and improve overall operational efficiency. By embracing the science behind demand forecasting, businesses can make informed decisions and thrive in today's dynamic marketplace.

Benefits of Demand Forecasting

Subchapter: Benefits of Demand Forecasting

Demand forecasting is a crucial aspect of operations and supply chain management that enables businesses to anticipate future demand for their products or services. In this subchapter, we will explore the numerous benefits that demand forecasting brings to organizations across various industries. Whether you are a business owner, a supply chain manager, or simply curious about the science behind demand forecasting, this section will shed light on the advantages it offers.

1. Enhanced Planning and Decision-making: Demand forecasting provides valuable insights into future market trends and customer preferences. By analyzing historical data, market research, and industry trends, businesses can make informed decisions about production, inventory management, and marketing strategies. This allows them to optimize their resources, minimize stockouts, reduce waste, and allocate budgets effectively.

2. Improved Inventory Management: Accurate demand forecasting aids in maintaining optimal inventory levels. It helps businesses avoid overstocking, which ties up capital and increases storage costs, while also preventing out-of-stock situations that lead to lost sales and dissatisfied customers. By aligning production and procurement with anticipated demand, businesses can achieve a balance between supply and demand, reducing carrying costs and maximizing profitability.

3. Efficient Supply Chain Management: Demand forecasting enables organizations to streamline their supply chain operations. By anticipating demand patterns, businesses can optimize production schedules, transportation routes, and warehouse capacities. This leads

to improved efficiency, reduced lead times, and enhanced customer satisfaction. Moreover, accurate forecasting enables businesses to collaborate effectively with suppliers, ensuring timely deliveries and minimizing disruptions.

4. Cost Savings: Demand forecasting helps organizations save money in various ways. By accurately predicting demand, businesses can avoid rush production or last-minute procurements, which often come at a premium cost. Additionally, optimized inventory management reduces storage costs, minimizes waste, and prevents obsolescence. By eliminating guesswork and basing decisions on data-driven insights, businesses can minimize costs and maximize profits.

5. Competitive Advantage: Businesses that excel in demand forecasting gain a competitive edge in the market. Accurately predicting customer demand allows organizations to respond swiftly to changing market conditions and customer preferences. This agility enables them to introduce new products or services, tailor marketing campaigns, and outperform competitors. Ultimately, demand forecasting empowers businesses to stay ahead of the curve and maintain a strong market position.

In conclusion, demand forecasting offers a plethora of benefits for organizations engaged in operations and supply chain management. From improved planning and decision-making to efficient inventory and supply chain management, demand forecasting plays a pivotal role in driving profitability, reducing costs, and gaining a competitive advantage. By embracing the science behind demand forecasting, businesses can navigate the ever-changing market dynamics with confidence and achieve long-term success.

Challenges in Demand Forecasting

In the dynamic world of operations and supply chain management, demand forecasting plays a crucial role in ensuring product availability and customer satisfaction. However, it is not without its fair share of challenges. This subchapter explores some of the key challenges that arise in demand forecasting and provides a layman's perspective on how to address them.

One of the primary challenges in demand forecasting is the accuracy of data. Forecasting relies heavily on historical data, and any inaccuracies or gaps in this data can significantly impact the accuracy of the forecast. Moreover, the availability of accurate and reliable data can be a challenge in itself, as data collection processes may be flawed or incomplete. To overcome this challenge, organizations must invest in robust data collection systems and ensure data integrity through regular audits and validation.

Another significant challenge in demand forecasting is the presence of outliers or anomalies in the data. These outliers can distort the forecast and lead to inaccurate predictions. It is essential to identify and remove such outliers before forecasting to ensure the reliability of the results. This can be achieved by using statistical methods or advanced analytics techniques to detect and handle outliers effectively.

Seasonality is yet another challenge in demand forecasting. Many products exhibit distinct seasonal patterns, making it difficult to accurately forecast demand throughout the year. Without accounting for seasonality, organizations may end up with excess inventory during off-peak seasons or face stockouts during peak seasons. Addressing this challenge requires the use of sophisticated forecasting models that can capture and incorporate seasonal patterns accurately.

Additionally, demand forecasting is also susceptible to external factors that are beyond the control of organizations. These factors, such as economic conditions, natural disasters, or sudden market disruptions, can significantly impact customer demand. To mitigate the impact of external factors, organizations must continuously monitor and analyze market trends, collaborate with suppliers and customers, and be prepared to adapt their forecasting models and strategies accordingly.

In conclusion, demand forecasting is a critical component of operations and supply chain management. However, it is not without its challenges. Accuracy of data, outliers, seasonality, and external factors all pose significant hurdles in achieving reliable demand forecasts. By understanding and addressing these challenges, organizations can enhance their forecasting capabilities and make informed decisions to optimize their operations and meet customer demand effectively.

Chapter 2: Understanding the Basics

Factors Affecting Demand

In the field of operations and supply chain management, understanding the factors that influence demand is crucial for accurate demand forecasting. Demand forecasting plays a key role in businesses, enabling them to make informed decisions regarding production levels, inventory management, and resource allocation. Consequently, a comprehensive understanding of the factors affecting demand is essential for any organization seeking to optimize their operations.

One of the primary factors that influence demand is consumer behavior. Consumer preferences, habits, and buying patterns can significantly impact the demand for a product or service. As consumer tastes change over time, businesses must adapt their offerings to meet these evolving demands. Factors such as income levels, demographics, and cultural influences also play a role in shaping consumer behavior and subsequently affect demand.

Economic conditions are another critical factor affecting demand. During periods of economic growth, consumer spending tends to increase, resulting in higher demand for products and services. Conversely, during economic downturns, consumers may tighten their budgets, leading to a decrease in demand. Understanding these economic trends and their impact on demand is crucial for businesses to effectively plan their operations and adjust their strategies accordingly.

External factors such as government regulations, technological advancements, and competitive forces also influence demand.

Government policies and regulations can directly impact demand by imposing restrictions or providing incentives for certain products or industries. Technological advancements, on the other hand, can create entirely new markets or render existing products obsolete, significantly altering demand patterns. Additionally, competitive forces within the market can shape demand as businesses strive to differentiate themselves and capture market share.

Lastly, seasonality and trends affect demand in various industries. For example, the demand for winter clothing typically increases during colder months, while demand for swimwear peaks during summer. Similarly, certain industries experience trends that affect demand, such as the increasing demand for sustainable and eco-friendly products. Recognizing and accounting for these seasonal patterns and trends is crucial for accurate demand forecasting and effective supply chain management.

In conclusion, numerous factors influence demand in the field of operations and supply chain management. Understanding consumer behavior, economic conditions, external forces, and industry-specific factors is essential for accurate demand forecasting and successful operations. By considering these factors, businesses can optimize their resource allocation, improve inventory management, and ultimately enhance their overall operational efficiency.

Types of Demand Forecasting

In the world of operations and supply chain management, demand forecasting plays a crucial role in determining the future needs of customers. It involves analyzing historical data, market trends, and consumer behavior to predict the demand for products or services in the future. In this subchapter, we will explore the various types of demand forecasting methods that are commonly used by businesses to make informed decisions.

1. Qualitative Forecasting: Qualitative forecasting methods rely on expert opinions, market research, and subjective information to predict future demand. These methods are often used in situations where historical data is limited or unreliable. Techniques such as the Delphi method, market surveys, and panel consensus are employed to gather insights from industry experts, customers, and stakeholders.

2. Time Series Analysis: Time series analysis is a quantitative method that uses historical data to predict future demand. It assumes that future patterns and trends can be identified by analyzing past behavior. This method is suitable for businesses with a long history of reliable data. Techniques like moving averages, exponential smoothing, and trend analysis are employed to identify patterns and extrapolate future demand.

3. Causal Forecasting: Causal forecasting looks beyond historical data and considers external factors that may influence demand. It examines the relationship between demand and various causal factors such as price changes, economic indicators, or changes in consumer behavior. Regression analysis, econometric models, and simulation techniques are

commonly used in this method to determine the impact of these factors on future demand.

4.   Judgmental   Forecasting: Judgmental forecasting is a combination of qualitative and quantitative methods. It involves incorporating expert opinions and insights from managers, sales representatives, and other relevant individuals. This method is particularly useful when dealing with new products, market disruptions, or rapidly changing customer preferences.

5.   Demand   Planning   Software: Advancements in technology have led to the development of sophisticated demand planning software. These tools utilize machine learning algorithms, artificial intelligence, and big data analytics to forecast demand accurately. They can process vast amounts of data, identify patterns, and make real-time adjustments based on market dynamics, enabling businesses to optimize their supply chain operations.

In conclusion, demand forecasting is a critical aspect of operations and supply chain management. By using various forecasting methods such as qualitative, time series analysis, causal, judgmental, and leveraging advanced demand planning software, businesses can make informed decisions and optimize their operations to meet the future needs of customers. It is essential for organizations to choose the most appropriate forecasting method based on their industry, available data, and specific requirements.

Qualitative Forecasting Methods

In the field of Operations and Supply Chain Management, forecasting plays a crucial role in making informed decisions about future demand. While quantitative forecasting methods rely heavily on historical data and mathematical models, qualitative forecasting methods provide valuable insights when data is limited or unavailable. This subchapter delves into the world of qualitative forecasting methods, exploring their significance and applicability in various business scenarios.

Qualitative forecasting methods are subjective techniques that rely on expert opinions, intuition, and judgment to predict future demand. These methods are particularly useful when there is a lack of historical data or when the market is experiencing significant changes, such as the introduction of a new product, changes in consumer preferences, or economic shifts. By utilizing the knowledge and expertise of individuals within an organization or industry, qualitative forecasting methods can provide valuable insights that complement quantitative approaches.

One commonly used qualitative forecasting method is the Delphi method. This approach involves gathering a panel of experts who provide their individual forecasts anonymously. The forecasts are then aggregated, and the panel members are given the opportunity to revise their predictions based on the group's feedback. This iterative process continues until a consensus is reached. The Delphi method helps eliminate personal biases and ensures a more accurate forecast by leveraging the collective wisdom of the experts.

Another qualitative forecasting method is scenario analysis. This technique involves developing multiple scenarios based on different assumptions about the future. Each scenario represents a plausible future state, considering various internal and external factors. By analyzing these scenarios, decision-makers can identify potential risks and opportunities, allowing them to make more informed decisions and develop contingency plans.

Qualitative forecasting methods also include market research techniques, such as surveys, focus groups, and customer feedback. These methods enable organizations to gather valuable insights directly from their target audience, helping them understand customer preferences, anticipate trends, and identify potential demand drivers.

While qualitative forecasting methods may not provide precise numerical predictions like their quantitative counterparts, they offer valuable qualitative insights that can inform decision-making processes. By leveraging the expertise of individuals, considering multiple scenarios, and gathering market research data, organizations can enhance their forecasting accuracy and make better informed business decisions.

In conclusion, qualitative forecasting methods are essential tools in the Operations and Supply Chain Management field. They offer valuable insights that complement quantitative approaches, especially in situations where historical data is limited or the market is undergoing significant changes. By utilizing techniques such as the Delphi method, scenario analysis, and market research, organizations can better anticipate future demand and make informed decisions that drive their success in a rapidly changing business environment.

Quantitative Forecasting Methods

In the field of Operations and Supply Chain Management, accurate demand forecasting is crucial for effective planning and decision-making. It enables organizations to optimize their inventory levels, production schedules, and distribution networks. Quantitative forecasting methods, based on historical data and mathematical models, play a pivotal role in providing reliable estimates of future demand patterns. In this subchapter, we will delve into the key techniques and concepts behind these methods to shed light on the science of demand forecasting.

One of the fundamental quantitative forecasting methods is the Time Series Analysis. It involves examining patterns and trends in historical data to project future demand. Techniques such as moving averages, exponential smoothing, and trend analysis are utilized to identify and capture different components of the time series, including seasonality, cyclical variations, and random fluctuations. This approach is particularly useful when historical data is abundant and there is a stable pattern to analyze.

Another widely-used quantitative method is Regression Analysis. By establishing a relationship between the demand variable and various influencing factors, regression models can be developed to predict future demand. Multiple regression allows for the consideration of multiple independent variables, enabling a more comprehensive analysis of demand drivers. This method is particularly valuable when there are clear cause-and-effect relationships that can be quantified.

In addition, we explore the concept of Forecast Accuracy, which measures the extent to which the forecasted values align with the actual demand. Various metrics, such as Mean Absolute Percentage

Error (MAPE) and Mean Squared Error (MSE), are employed to evaluate the accuracy of the forecasting models. Understanding forecast accuracy is crucial as it helps organizations gauge the reliability of their forecasts and make informed decisions accordingly.

While quantitative forecasting methods provide valuable insights, it is important to acknowledge their limitations. These methods assume that historical patterns will continue to hold true in the future, which may not always be the case. Exogenous factors, such as changes in market conditions or disruptive innovations, can significantly impact demand and render historical data less relevant. Therefore, it is essential to supplement quantitative methods with qualitative judgment and expert opinion to develop a holistic and robust forecasting approach.

In conclusion, quantitative forecasting methods offer valuable tools for Operations and Supply Chain Management professionals to predict future demand patterns. By leveraging historical data and mathematical models, organizations can make informed decisions about inventory planning, production scheduling, and distribution strategies. However, it is crucial to recognize the limitations of these methods and combine them with qualitative insights to develop accurate and reliable demand forecasts.

Key Metrics in Demand Forecasting

In the world of operations and supply chain management, demand forecasting plays a pivotal role in ensuring the smooth functioning of businesses. By accurately predicting customer demand, companies can optimize their inventory levels, production schedules, and overall supply chain activities. However, the science behind demand forecasting can be complex and overwhelming for those not well-versed in the field. This subchapter aims to provide a layman's perspective on key metrics used in demand forecasting to help everyone understand the fundamental concepts and make informed decisions.

1. Forecast Accuracy: Forecast accuracy is a crucial metric that measures the extent to which a forecast aligns with actual demand. By comparing historical data with forecasted values, companies can assess the reliability of their forecasting methods. High forecast accuracy indicates the ability to anticipate customer demand effectively, leading to improved decision-making and reduced costs.

2. Mean Absolute Percentage Error (MAPE): MAPE is a widely used metric that measures the accuracy of a forecast by calculating the average percentage difference between actual and forecasted values. It provides a standardized way to compare forecast performance across different products or time periods. A lower MAPE indicates higher forecast accuracy, while a higher MAPE suggests a less reliable forecast.

3. Forecast Bias: Forecast bias refers to the tendency of a forecast to consistently overestimate or underestimate actual demand. It is essential to

monitor and minimize forecast bias to avoid unnecessary inventory costs or stockouts. A neutral or unbiased forecast is ideal, as it indicates an accurate prediction of future demand.

4. Forecast Horizon: The forecast horizon refers to the time period for which a demand forecast is generated. Short-term forecasts typically cover a few weeks or months, while long-term forecasts may span several years. Understanding the forecast horizon is crucial for aligning production schedules, inventory management, and resource allocation.

5. Forecast Error Distribution: Analyzing the distribution of forecast errors helps identify patterns in forecasting accuracy. Common error distributions include normal, skewed, or bimodal. By understanding the distribution of errors, businesses can fine-tune their forecasting models and make adjustments to improve accuracy.

6. Demand Variability: Demand variability measures the extent to which demand fluctuates over time. High demand variability requires more sophisticated forecasting techniques and increased safety stock levels to mitigate the risk of stockouts. Understanding demand variability helps businesses adapt their supply chain strategies to handle fluctuations effectively.

In conclusion, mastering the key metrics in demand forecasting is vital for operations and supply chain management professionals. Forecast accuracy, MAPE, forecast bias, forecast horizon, forecast error distribution, and demand variability are fundamental concepts that can guide decision-making and optimize supply chain activities. By employing these metrics, businesses can improve their forecasting capabilities, reduce costs, enhance customer satisfaction, and gain a competitive edge in the market.

Sales Forecasting

Sales forecasting is a crucial aspect of operations and supply chain management, as it allows businesses to anticipate future customer demand and make informed decisions about production, inventory, and resource allocation. In this subchapter, we will delve into the science behind sales forecasting and explore its significance in driving business success.

Sales forecasting refers to the process of estimating future sales levels based on historical data, market trends, and other relevant factors. It involves analyzing past sales patterns, understanding market conditions, and considering external factors such as economic indicators, consumer behavior, and competition. By predicting sales volumes accurately, businesses can align their operations to meet anticipated demand efficiently.

One of the primary benefits of sales forecasting is that it enables businesses to optimize their inventory management. By forecasting future sales, companies can adjust their inventory levels accordingly, minimizing the risk of stockouts or excess inventory. This, in turn, leads to improved customer satisfaction, reduced carrying costs, and increased profitability.

Furthermore, sales forecasting plays a crucial role in production planning and capacity management. By accurately predicting sales volumes, businesses can plan their production schedules, allocate resources, and optimize their production capabilities. This prevents underutilization or overutilization of resources, streamlines operations, and enhances overall efficiency.

Sales forecasting also aids in decision-making related to marketing and promotions. By understanding future demand, businesses can strategically plan their marketing campaigns, allocate budgets, and target the right customer segments. This helps maximize the return on marketing investments and ensures that promotional efforts align with expected sales volumes.

However, it is essential to note that sales forecasting is not an exact science. It relies on historical data and assumptions about future market conditions, which may not always be accurate. Factors such as unexpected changes in consumer behavior, economic fluctuations, or industry disruptions can significantly impact sales forecasts. Therefore, businesses must regularly review and update their forecasts to adapt to changing market dynamics.

In conclusion, sales forecasting is a vital tool for operations and supply chain management. It enables businesses to make informed decisions about inventory management, production planning, and marketing strategies. While it may not be foolproof, a well-executed sales forecasting process can significantly enhance a company's ability to meet customer demand, minimize costs, and drive overall business success.

Market Research Analysis

Market research analysis is a crucial component of operations and supply chain management that allows businesses to gain valuable insights into consumer behavior, preferences, and market trends. By understanding the dynamics of the market, companies can make informed decisions, develop effective strategies, and improve their overall performance.

In this subchapter, we will explore the science behind market research analysis and its significance in demand forecasting. Whether you are a business owner, a professional in operations and supply chain management, or simply curious about the subject, this section aims to provide you with a layman's perspective on this essential aspect of running a successful business.

Market research analysis involves gathering and interpreting data from various sources to understand consumer needs, expectations, and purchasing patterns. This data is collected through surveys, interviews, focus groups, and other research methods. By analyzing this information, businesses can identify emerging trends, evaluate their target market, and evaluate the potential demand for their products or services.

One of the primary goals of market research analysis is to identify and understand customer segments. By dividing the market into distinct groups based on demographics, psychographics, or behavioral characteristics, businesses can tailor their marketing strategies to meet the specific needs of each segment. This targeted approach not only improves customer satisfaction but also increases the likelihood of capturing a larger market share.

Furthermore, market research analysis helps businesses stay ahead of the competition. By constantly monitoring the market, companies can identify new competitors, evaluate their strengths and weaknesses, and adjust their strategies accordingly. This proactive approach enables businesses to anticipate changes in the market, adapt their operations, and maintain a competitive edge.

Additionally, market research analysis plays a vital role in product development and innovation. By understanding consumer preferences and needs, businesses can identify opportunities for new product development or improvements to existing products. This data-driven approach minimizes the risk of launching unsuccessful products and maximizes the chances of meeting customer expectations.

In conclusion, market research analysis is an indispensable tool for businesses operating in the field of operations and supply chain management. By understanding the science behind this practice, companies can make informed decisions, develop effective strategies, and achieve sustainable growth. Whether you are a business owner or a professional in the industry, mastering the art of market research analysis is essential for success in today's competitive market.

Customer Segmentation

In the fast-paced world of business, understanding your customers is crucial to success. Customer segmentation, a powerful tool in the realm of operations and supply chain management, is the process of dividing your target market into distinct groups based on their unique characteristics, needs, and behaviors. By segmenting your customers, you can develop tailored strategies that resonate with each group, resulting in increased customer satisfaction, loyalty, and ultimately, profitability.

In today's diverse marketplace, one size does not fit all. Every customer is different, and their preferences, purchasing habits, and motivations vary greatly. Customer segmentation allows you to identify these differences and create targeted marketing campaigns, personalized product offerings, and exceptional customer experiences. By understanding the specific needs and desires of each segment, you can effectively allocate resources, optimize your supply chain, and streamline your operations.

There are various ways to segment customers, depending on your industry and business goals. Demographic segmentation involves categorizing customers based on age, gender, income, education, and other demographic factors. This approach enables you to target specific age groups or income brackets, tailoring your products and marketing messages accordingly. Psychographic segmentation, on the other hand, focuses on customers' attitudes, values, interests, and lifestyles. By understanding their motivations and preferences, you can create marketing campaigns that resonate on a deeper level.

Another popular segmentation approach is behavioral segmentation, which groups customers based on their purchasing patterns, brand loyalty, usage frequency, and other behavioral aspects. This method allows you to identify your most valuable customers, develop loyalty programs, and drive repeat purchases. Geographic segmentation, meanwhile, divides customers based on their geographic location, enabling you to customize your offerings to suit regional preferences and trends.

Customer segmentation is not a one-time process but rather an ongoing effort. As customer preferences and market dynamics evolve, so should your segmentation strategies. By regularly analyzing data, conducting surveys, and monitoring market trends, you can identify emerging segments, refine your existing ones, and adapt your business strategies accordingly.

In conclusion, customer segmentation is a vital tool for operations and supply chain management. It empowers businesses to understand their customers at a deeper level and tailor their strategies to meet their unique needs. By segmenting customers, you can optimize your supply chain, allocate resources effectively, and drive customer loyalty. Whether you are in retail, manufacturing, or any other industry, customer segmentation is an essential practice that can unlock growth and success in today's competitive marketplace.

Chapter 3: Demand Forecasting Techniques

Moving Averages

In the realm of operations and supply chain management, accurate demand forecasting is crucial for effective planning, inventory management, and production scheduling. One popular and widely used technique for demand forecasting is the moving averages method. This subchapter aims to shed light on the science behind moving averages and how it can be applied to improve forecasting accuracy.

Moving averages, as the name suggests, involves calculating the average of a series of data points over a specified period. It is particularly useful when dealing with time series data, where historical demand patterns play a significant role in predicting future demand. By smoothing out short-term fluctuations, moving averages provide a clearer picture of the underlying demand trend.

There are various types of moving averages, such as simple moving average (SMA), weighted moving average (WMA), and exponential moving average (EMA). Each type offers its unique advantages and is suitable for different forecasting scenarios. However, the basic principle remains the same – to estimate future demand based on past data.

The simplicity and ease of calculation make moving averages an attractive method for demand forecasting. It requires minimal mathematical expertise and can be implemented using spreadsheet software. By choosing an appropriate time frame for the moving average, analysts can strike a balance between responsiveness to recent changes and stability in capturing overall trends.

However, it is important to note that moving averages have limitations. They assume that historical demand patterns will continue in the future, neglecting any external factors that could impact demand. Additionally, moving averages may not be suitable for capturing sudden demand fluctuations or seasonality. Therefore, it is advisable to combine moving averages with other forecasting techniques to enhance accuracy and account for these limitations.

In conclusion, moving averages are a valuable tool in the arsenal of operations and supply chain management professionals. They provide a simple yet effective method for demand forecasting, enabling businesses to make informed decisions regarding production, inventory, and resource allocation. While they may not be the ultimate solution for all forecasting challenges, moving averages serve as a solid foundation for understanding and predicting demand trends. By harnessing the power of moving averages, businesses can optimize their operations and stay ahead in today's competitive market.

Weighted Moving Averages

In the realm of operations and supply chain management, accurate demand forecasting is crucial for effective planning and decision-making. One widely used technique in demand forecasting is the Weighted Moving Averages method. This subchapter aims to provide a comprehensive understanding of this technique, its principles, and how it can be applied in various contexts.

The Weighted Moving Averages method is an extension of the simple Moving Averages technique, which calculates the average of a series of data points over a specified time period. However, unlike the simple Moving Averages, the Weighted Moving Averages assigns different weights to each data point based on their relative importance or significance. This allows for a more precise and tailored forecasting approach.

The underlying principle of the Weighted Moving Averages lies in the assumption that recent data points are more relevant and influential in predicting future demand than older ones. By assigning higher weights to recent data points, the method captures the evolving trends and patterns in demand more effectively. The weights can be determined based on expert judgment, historical data analysis, or statistical methods.

One advantage of the Weighted Moving Averages method is its flexibility. It can be customized to suit different business contexts, such as seasonal demand patterns or product-specific characteristics. For instance, a company experiencing significant fluctuations in demand during certain times of the year can assign higher weights to data points from those periods to better capture the seasonal variations.

Implementing the Weighted Moving Averages method requires a systematic approach. First, the appropriate time period for the moving average needs to be determined, considering factors such as product lifecycle, market dynamics, and business objectives. Then, the weights for each data point within the chosen time period should be assigned. Finally, the weighted average is calculated, providing a forecast for future demand.

It is important to note that the Weighted Moving Averages method has its limitations. It assumes that the factors influencing demand remain constant over time and does not account for sudden changes or external events. Additionally, the accuracy of the forecasts heavily relies on the quality and availability of data.

Overall, the Weighted Moving Averages method is a valuable tool in demand forecasting for operations and supply chain management. By incorporating recent data points with higher weights, this technique provides a more accurate prediction of future demand, allowing businesses to make informed decisions and optimize their planning processes.

Exponential Smoothing

Exponential smoothing is a widely used technique in the field of demand forecasting that helps businesses predict future demand patterns effectively. It is a mathematical method that assigns exponentially decreasing weights to past observations, emphasizing recent data and diminishing the importance of older data. This approach is particularly useful in capturing short-term fluctuations while still taking into account the overall trend in demand.

In the realm of operations and supply chain management, accurate demand forecasting is crucial for optimizing inventory levels, production planning, and resource allocation. By employing exponential smoothing, businesses can make informed decisions based on reliable projections, enhancing operational efficiency and customer satisfaction.

The basic principle behind exponential smoothing is the assumption that recent data points are more indicative of future demand compared to older data points. The technique calculates the forecasted demand by combining the most recent observation with a fraction of the error from the previous forecast. The fraction, often referred to as the smoothing constant, determines the weight assigned to the previous forecast error. A higher smoothing constant gives more weight to recent observations, resulting in a greater responsiveness to changes in demand.

There are various types of exponential smoothing methods, each suited for different demand patterns. Simple exponential smoothing is the most basic form, suitable for stable and consistent demand. It assigns equal weight to all past observations and is ideal when there are no apparent trends or seasonality in the data.

On the other hand, Holt's linear exponential smoothing method incorporates trend information in addition to the base level of demand. This method is suitable when the demand exhibits a consistent upward or downward trend over time. By considering both the base level and the trend, Holt's method provides a more accurate forecast than simple exponential smoothing alone.

Another popular technique, Holt-Winters' exponential smoothing, accounts for both trend and seasonality in demand patterns. By considering the seasonality factor, this method is particularly useful for industries with distinct seasonal variations. It enables businesses to anticipate demand fluctuations during specific periods and adjust their operations accordingly.

In conclusion, exponential smoothing is a powerful tool in demand forecasting, allowing businesses in the fields of operations and supply chain management to make informed decisions based on accurate predictions. By capturing short-term fluctuations while considering long-term trends, exponential smoothing helps optimize inventory levels, streamline production planning, and allocate resources efficiently. Regardless of industry, understanding and implementing exponential smoothing techniques can significantly enhance a company's operational performance and overall competitiveness in the market.

Regression Analysis

Regression analysis is a powerful statistical technique that is widely used in various fields, including operations and supply chain management. It helps in understanding the relationship between a dependent variable and one or more independent variables. In the context of demand forecasting, regression analysis can be a valuable tool for predicting future demand based on historical data and other relevant factors.

The fundamental concept behind regression analysis is to identify and quantify the relationship between variables. In the case of demand forecasting, the dependent variable is typically the demand for a product or service, while the independent variables can include factors such as price, advertising expenditure, seasonality, and competitor activities. By analyzing historical data containing these variables, regression analysis can provide insights into how changes in the independent variables affect the dependent variable.

One of the main benefits of regression analysis is its ability to generate forecasts by considering multiple factors simultaneously. Instead of relying on a single variable, regression analysis allows us to incorporate various independent variables that may influence demand. By doing so, we can create a more accurate and reliable forecast that takes into account the complex dynamics of the marketplace.

There are different types of regression analysis techniques, such as simple linear regression, multiple linear regression, and logistic regression, each suited for specific types of data and research questions. Simple linear regression, for example, is used when there is a linear relationship between the dependent and independent variables. Multiple linear regression, on the other hand, is applicable when there are multiple independent variables involved.

To conduct regression analysis, statistical software tools are commonly used. These tools automate the complex calculations involved in regression analysis, making it easier for practitioners to analyze large datasets efficiently. However, it is important to interpret the results carefully and consider the limitations of the analysis.

Regression analysis is not without its limitations. It assumes that the relationship between the dependent and independent variables is linear and does not account for complex interactions or non-linear relationships. Additionally, it assumes that the historical data used for analysis is representative of future trends, which may not always be the case.

Despite these limitations, regression analysis remains a valuable tool in the field of demand forecasting. By understanding the relationship between various factors and demand, organizations can make informed decisions regarding pricing, marketing strategies, and production planning. It enables businesses to optimize their operations and supply chain management by aligning their resources with anticipated demand patterns.

In conclusion, regression analysis is a powerful technique that provides insights into the relationship between variables, particularly in the context of demand forecasting. By analyzing historical data and other relevant factors, regression analysis enables organizations to generate accurate forecasts and make informed decisions. While it has its limitations, when used appropriately, regression analysis can be a valuable tool for improving operations and supply chain management.

Time Series Analysis

In the world of operations and supply chain management, making accurate demand forecasts is crucial for effective decision-making and planning. One powerful tool that helps in this endeavor is time series analysis. This subchapter will introduce the concept of time series analysis and its relevance in forecasting demand.

Time series analysis is a statistical technique that allows us to analyze and interpret patterns in data collected over time. It involves studying the past behavior of a variable to make predictions and understand its future trends. In the context of demand forecasting, time series analysis enables us to uncover patterns and relationships that exist within historical demand data.

Why is time series analysis important? Well, the demand for products and services is influenced by various factors such as seasonality, trends, and external events. By understanding these patterns, businesses can make informed decisions regarding production levels, inventory management, and resource allocation. Time series analysis provides a framework to identify and quantify these patterns, allowing organizations to optimize their operations and supply chain management effectively.

There are several methods and models employed in time series analysis. One common technique is moving averages, which smooth out fluctuations in data to identify underlying trends. Another approach is exponential smoothing, which assigns more weight to recent observations and less to older ones, allowing for better sensitivity to recent changes in demand.

In addition to these techniques, time series analysis also encompasses more advanced models such as autoregressive integrated moving average (ARIMA) and seasonal decomposition of time series (STL). These models capture complex relationships within the data and provide accurate forecasts for future demand.

It is important to note that time series analysis is not a crystal ball that predicts the future with certainty. However, it provides valuable insights and helps decision-makers make informed judgments based on historical patterns and trends. By leveraging time series analysis, businesses can improve their forecasting accuracy, streamline their supply chains, and enhance overall operational efficiency.

In conclusion, time series analysis is a fundamental tool for operations and supply chain management professionals. It enables businesses to uncover patterns and trends within historical demand data, leading to more accurate forecasts and better decision-making. By embracing the science behind demand forecasting, organizations can gain a competitive edge in today's rapidly changing business landscape.

Causal Models

In the realm of Operations and Supply Chain Management, accurate demand forecasting is crucial for businesses to effectively plan their production and inventory levels. Causal models play a pivotal role in this process, providing insights into the relationships between various factors that influence demand.

Causal models enable businesses to understand the cause-and-effect relationships that exist within their operations. By analyzing historical data and identifying patterns, these models help uncover the factors that directly impact demand. This information allows businesses to make informed decisions and develop strategies to optimize their supply chain processes.

One of the key advantages of causal models is their ability to incorporate external factors that influence demand. These factors, such as economic indicators, market trends, and even weather patterns, can significantly impact consumer behavior and subsequently affect demand. Causal models help businesses account for these external variables, enabling them to make more accurate forecasts and mitigate potential risks.

There are various types of causal models, each with its own unique approach. Time series analysis, for example, examines historical demand patterns to identify trends and seasonality. By understanding these patterns, businesses can anticipate fluctuations in demand and align their production and inventory levels accordingly.

Another type of causal model is regression analysis, which seeks to establish relationships between the dependent variable (demand) and multiple independent variables (such as price, promotions, and competitor activity). Regression analysis helps businesses quantify the impact of each independent variable on demand, allowing them to prioritize and optimize their marketing and pricing strategies.

Furthermore, advanced causal models, such as econometric models and simulation models, offer businesses the ability to simulate various scenarios and predict the potential outcome on demand. These models are particularly useful for strategic decision-making, as they allow businesses to assess the impact of potential changes in factors such as pricing, product features, or market conditions.

In summary, causal models provide businesses with a scientific approach to demand forecasting. By uncovering the relationships between various factors that influence demand, businesses can make data-driven decisions and optimize their supply chain processes. Whether it is identifying seasonality, quantifying the impact of marketing activities, or simulating different scenarios, causal models are an invaluable tool for businesses in the field of Operations and Supply Chain Management.

Chapter 4: Data Collection and Analysis

Data Sources for Demand Forecasting

In the world of operations and supply chain management, accurate demand forecasting is crucial for effective planning and decision-making. It enables companies to optimize inventory levels, allocate resources efficiently, and meet customer demands promptly. However, the process of demand forecasting heavily relies on the availability of reliable and comprehensive data sources. In this subchapter, we will explore the various data sources that play a significant role in demand forecasting.

Historical Sales Data: One of the primary sources of data for demand forecasting is historical sales data. This data provides valuable insights into past purchasing patterns and can be used to identify trends, seasonality, and other patterns that can help predict future demand. By analyzing historical sales data, companies can identify the factors that influence demand and develop accurate forecasts.

Customer Surveys and Feedback: Understanding customer preferences and behavior is essential for demand forecasting. Customer surveys and feedback provide valuable information about their needs, preferences, and purchasing patterns. By collecting and analyzing this data, companies can gain insights into customer sentiment, identify emerging trends, and adjust their forecasts accordingly.

Market Research and Industry Reports: Market research and industry reports offer valuable data on market trends, competitor analysis, and industry dynamics. These reports provide insights into consumer behavior, market size, and growth potential, enabling companies to make informed decisions about their demand forecasting strategies.

Point of Sale (POS) Data: Point of sale data provides real-time information about customer purchases, allowing companies to track sales patterns and adjust forecasts accordingly. By collecting and analyzing POS data, businesses can identify changes in demand, detect stockouts or excess inventory, and optimize their supply chain processes.

External Data Sources: In addition to internal data sources, external data can also contribute to accurate demand forecasting. This includes data from weather forecasts, economic indicators, social media trends, and other external factors that can impact consumer behavior. By incorporating external data sources into their forecasting models, companies can improve the accuracy of their predictions and respond effectively to changing market conditions.

It is essential for companies to leverage a combination of these data sources to enhance their demand forecasting capabilities. By utilizing historical sales data, customer surveys, market research, point of sale data, and external data sources, companies can develop more accurate and reliable demand forecasts. This, in turn, allows them to optimize their operations, improve customer satisfaction, and gain a competitive edge in the market.

In conclusion, demand forecasting is a critical aspect of operations and supply chain management. By using a wide range of data sources, companies can enhance their forecasting accuracy and make informed decisions that drive organizational success.

Internal Data Sources

In the world of operations and supply chain management, accurate demand forecasting is crucial for optimizing resources, maximizing efficiency, and ultimately driving business success. To achieve accurate forecasts, businesses rely on a variety of data sources, both internal and external. In this subchapter, we will delve into the realm of internal data sources and explore their significance in the science of demand forecasting.

Internal data sources refer to the data generated within an organization. These sources are unique to each business, as they comprise data collected from its own operations, sales, and customer interactions. Leveraging internal data sources is fundamental for organizations to gain insights into their own historical performance, trends, and patterns. By analyzing this data, businesses can make informed decisions about future demand and plan their operations accordingly.

One of the primary internal data sources for demand forecasting is sales data. This data provides a wealth of information about the organization's past sales performance, including product/service demand, seasonal variations, and customer preferences. Analyzing sales data can help identify trends and patterns, enabling businesses to forecast future demand more accurately. Additionally, sales data can be segmented to gain insights into different customer groups, geographic regions, or product categories, further enhancing the forecasting process.

Apart from sales data, inventory data is another crucial internal data source. Tracking inventory levels provides valuable information about product availability, stockouts, and replenishment patterns. By analyzing inventory data, businesses can identify the impact of stockouts on customer demand and optimize their inventory management strategies accordingly. This can help prevent lost sales opportunities due to insufficient stock, ultimately improving customer satisfaction and profitability.

Customer data is yet another essential internal data source for demand forecasting. By understanding customer behaviors, preferences, and purchase patterns, businesses can tailor their forecasting models to better anticipate future demand. Customer data can be collected through various channels, such as loyalty programs, surveys, or online interactions. Analyzing this data allows businesses to segment customers, personalize marketing strategies, and forecast demand at a granular level.

In conclusion, internal data sources play a vital role in the science of demand forecasting. By leveraging sales data, inventory data, and customer data, businesses can gain valuable insights into their own operations and make accurate predictions about future demand. These insights enable organizations to optimize their resources, streamline their supply chains, and ultimately drive business success. Therefore, understanding and harnessing internal data sources is crucial for any organization seeking to excel in operations and supply chain management.

External Data Sources

In the realm of operations and supply chain management, accurate demand forecasting is crucial for the success of any business. The ability to predict customer demand with precision allows companies to optimize their inventory levels, production schedules, and overall supply chain operations. However, relying solely on internal data sources may not provide a comprehensive understanding of the market dynamics and external factors that influence demand. This is where external data sources come into play.

External data sources refer to information obtained from outside the organization, often from third-party providers, that can enhance the accuracy and reliability of demand forecasting models. These sources provide valuable insights into market trends, consumer behavior, economic indicators, and other external factors that impact demand patterns.

One of the most commonly used external data sources is social media data. Social media platforms like Twitter, Facebook, and Instagram generate an enormous amount of user-generated content that can be analyzed to gain insights into consumer preferences, sentiment, and emerging trends. By monitoring social media conversations and analyzing the data, businesses can identify patterns and make informed decisions regarding product development, marketing campaigns, and demand forecasting.

Another valuable external data source is government data. Government agencies collect and publish data on various economic indicators, such as GDP growth, employment rates, inflation, and consumer spending. This data provides a macroeconomic perspective that can help businesses understand the overall economic climate and its potential impact on consumer demand. By incorporating government data into demand forecasting models, companies can anticipate changes in demand more accurately and adjust their strategies accordingly.

Furthermore, industry reports and market research studies conducted by specialized firms offer valuable insights into specific markets, consumer segments, and product categories. These reports provide data on market size, growth rates, competitive landscape, and consumer preferences, which can be used to refine demand forecasting models and make data-driven business decisions.

External data sources are not limited to the examples mentioned above. Depending on the industry and nature of the business, other relevant data sources may include weather data, competitor data, customer surveys, and more. The key is to identify and leverage the data sources that are most relevant to the specific business context.

In conclusion, external data sources play a crucial role in enhancing the accuracy and reliability of demand forecasting in operations and supply chain management. By incorporating data from social media, government sources, industry reports, and other relevant sources, businesses can gain valuable insights into market dynamics, consumer behavior, and external factors that influence demand. This enables them to make more informed decisions, optimize their supply chain operations, and stay ahead in the competitive marketplace.

Data Cleaning and Preprocessing

In the world of operations and supply chain management, accurate and reliable data is crucial for effective decision-making. However, raw data is often messy, inconsistent, and filled with errors, making it challenging to extract meaningful insights. This is where data cleaning and preprocessing come into play.

Data cleaning is the process of identifying and correcting or removing errors, inconsistencies, and inaccuracies in the dataset. It involves a series of techniques and algorithms to ensure that the data is reliable and ready for analysis. Preprocessing, on the other hand, involves transforming the data into a format that is suitable for analysis, such as standardizing variables or handling missing values.

Why is data cleaning and preprocessing important? The quality of the data directly impacts the accuracy and reliability of the insights derived from it. Garbage in, garbage out – if the data is flawed, any analysis or forecasting based on it will be equally flawed. By investing time and effort into cleaning and preprocessing the data, organizations can ensure that their decisions are based on accurate and reliable information.

Data cleaning involves several steps, including removing duplicates, handling missing values, correcting inconsistent values, and dealing with outliers. Duplicate records can skew the analysis and lead to incorrect conclusions, so it is essential to identify and remove them. Missing values, on the other hand, can cause biased results or incomplete analysis. Various techniques can be used to handle missing values, such as imputation or deleting the missing data.

Inconsistent values can arise due to human errors or different data sources. Standardization techniques can be applied to ensure that all variables are measured in the same units or scales. Outliers, which are extreme values that deviate significantly from the rest of the data, can also affect the analysis. It is crucial to identify and handle outliers appropriately to avoid their undue influence on the results.

Once the data is cleaned, preprocessing techniques can be applied to transform the data into a suitable format for analysis. This may involve normalizing or standardizing variables, encoding categorical variables, or reducing the dimensionality of the dataset.

In conclusion, data cleaning and preprocessing are fundamental steps in the journey of extracting meaningful insights from raw data. By investing time and effort into these processes, operations and supply chain management professionals can ensure that their decisions are based on accurate and reliable information. As the saying goes, "Clean data is happy data!"

Statistical Analysis Techniques

In the realm of operations and supply chain management, the importance of data analysis cannot be overstated. To make informed decisions and effectively forecast demand, professionals in these fields rely on statistical analysis techniques. This subchapter aims to introduce the key statistical analysis techniques used in demand forecasting, providing a layman's perspective for everyone interested in understanding the science behind it.

One of the fundamental statistical techniques employed in demand forecasting is time series analysis. Time series analysis examines data collected over a specific period and identifies patterns, trends, and seasonality. By analyzing historical demand data, professionals can make predictions about future demand patterns, enabling them to optimize inventory levels and production schedules. Techniques such as moving averages, exponential smoothing, and decomposition are commonly used in time series analysis.

Another statistical analysis technique widely used in operations and supply chain management is regression analysis. Regression analysis explores the relationship between a dependent variable (such as sales) and one or more independent variables (such as price, advertising expenditure, or economic indicators). By identifying the impact of various factors on demand, regression analysis helps forecast future demand scenarios. This technique enables professionals to determine the most influential variables and make data-driven decisions to optimize supply chain operations.

In addition to time series analysis and regression analysis, statistical techniques like cluster analysis and factor analysis are also valuable tools for demand forecasting. Cluster analysis groups similar demand patterns together, allowing businesses to tailor their strategies to different customer segments. On the other hand, factor analysis uncovers latent variables that contribute to demand variations, providing deeper insights into customer behavior and market dynamics.

While statistical analysis techniques provide valuable insights into future demand patterns, it is crucial to remember that they are not infallible. Demand forecasting involves uncertainties, and the accuracy of predictions may vary depending on various factors. Therefore, it is important to constantly evaluate and refine forecasting models based on new information and emerging trends.

In conclusion, statistical analysis techniques are essential tools in the field of operations and supply chain management. Time series analysis, regression analysis, cluster analysis, and factor analysis help professionals forecast demand, optimize inventory levels, and make data-driven decisions. By understanding these statistical techniques, individuals from every background can gain a layman's perspective on the science behind demand forecasting and contribute to the efficiency and success of their organizations.

Descriptive Statistics

In the field of Operations and Supply Chain Management, data plays a crucial role in decision-making processes. To effectively analyze and interpret this data, it is essential to have a solid understanding of descriptive statistics. This subchapter aims to introduce the concept of descriptive statistics and its significance in demand forecasting from a layman's perspective.

Descriptive statistics involves the collection, presentation, and analysis of data to summarize and describe its main characteristics. It provides a way to organize and understand large sets of data, making it easier to identify patterns, trends, and insights. By utilizing descriptive statistics techniques, businesses can gain valuable insights into their operations and supply chain management processes.

One of the primary uses of descriptive statistics in demand forecasting is to measure central tendency. This involves calculating various measures such as mean, median, and mode to determine the average value or typical value of a dataset. These measures help in understanding the average demand for a product or service, which is vital for inventory management and production planning.

Another important aspect of descriptive statistics is the measurement of dispersion. Measures like range, variance, and standard deviation provide information about the spread of data points around the central tendency. Understanding dispersion helps businesses assess the variability in demand, which can aid in setting safety stock levels and managing supply chain risks.

Graphical representation is an integral part of descriptive statistics. Visualizing data through charts, histograms, and scatter plots can provide a clearer understanding of patterns and trends. These visual representations allow decision-makers to identify outliers, seasonal patterns, and other factors that may impact demand forecasting accuracy.

Moreover, descriptive statistics also encompasses the calculation of percentiles and quartiles, which help in understanding the distribution of data and identifying potential demand segments. By segmenting the data based on percentiles, businesses can tailor their forecasting models to different customer segments, leading to more accurate predictions.

In summary, descriptive statistics is a powerful tool in the field of Operations and Supply Chain Management. By utilizing various measures and graphical representations, businesses can gain insights into their demand patterns, understand the variability, and make informed decisions regarding inventory management, production planning, and supply chain optimization. Understanding descriptive statistics is crucial for professionals in this field to effectively analyze data, improve forecasting accuracy, and ultimately enhance their overall operational efficiency.

Correlation Analysis

In the world of operations and supply chain management, making accurate demand forecasts is crucial to ensure the smooth functioning of businesses. However, predicting demand patterns can be a complex task, especially when dealing with various factors that influence consumer behavior. This is where correlation analysis comes into play, providing valuable insights into the relationship between different variables and their impact on demand forecasting.

Correlation analysis is a statistical technique that measures the strength and direction of the relationship between two or more variables. By analyzing historical data, businesses can identify patterns and trends that help them make informed decisions. This analysis enables them to understand how changes in one variable may affect another, ultimately leading to more accurate demand forecasts.

For instance, let's consider a manufacturing company that produces electronic gadgets. By conducting a correlation analysis, they may discover that there is a strong positive correlation between advertising expenditure and sales. This means that when they invest more in advertising, their sales tend to increase. Armed with this knowledge, the company can allocate their marketing budget more effectively to boost sales and meet demand.

Correlation analysis also helps in identifying variables that have a negative correlation. For example, a retailer may find that there is a negative correlation between price and demand for a particular product. This implies that when the price of the product increases, the demand decreases. By understanding this relationship, businesses can make pricing decisions that balance profitability and customer demand.

It is important to note that correlation does not imply causation. Just because two variables are correlated does not necessarily mean that one variable causes the other. However, correlation analysis provides a starting point for further investigation and understanding of the relationship between variables.

In addition to understanding the relationship between variables, correlation analysis also helps in measuring the strength of the relationship. The correlation coefficient, which ranges from -1 to +1, indicates the strength and direction of the relationship. A coefficient close to +1 indicates a strong positive correlation, while a coefficient close to -1 suggests a strong negative correlation. A coefficient close to zero indicates a weak or no correlation between the variables.

By utilizing correlation analysis in demand forecasting, businesses can make more informed decisions, optimize their operations, and minimize risks. It allows them to identify key factors that influence demand and adapt their strategies accordingly. Ultimately, correlation analysis empowers businesses to stay ahead in the competitive market by accurately predicting future demand patterns.

Hypothesis Testing

Hypothesis Testing: Unlocking the Secrets of Demand Forecasting

In the world of Operations and Supply Chain Management, accurate demand forecasting is a critical component for success. However, forecasting demand is not an exact science; it involves uncertainty and the need to make informed decisions based on available data. This is where hypothesis testing comes into play, providing a scientific approach to validate or reject assumptions about demand patterns.

Hypothesis testing is a statistical method that enables us to assess the validity of a claim or assumption about a population based on a sample. In the context of demand forecasting, it helps us determine whether a particular forecasting model or assumption is accurate and reliable. By applying hypothesis testing, we can make confident decisions about the reliability of our forecasts and adjust our strategies accordingly.

The process of hypothesis testing begins with the formulation of two competing hypotheses: the null hypothesis (H_0) and the alternative hypothesis (H_1). The null hypothesis represents the status quo or the assumption we want to test, while the alternative hypothesis presents an alternative claim or assumption. These hypotheses are then subjected to rigorous statistical analysis to assess their validity.

To conduct hypothesis testing in demand forecasting, we typically start by collecting a sample of historical demand data. This sample is then analyzed using statistical techniques to determine the probability of obtaining the observed results if the null hypothesis is true. This probability is known as the p-value, and it helps us make decisions about whether to reject or fail to reject the null hypothesis.

If the p-value is below a predetermined significance level (commonly set at 0.05), we reject the null hypothesis in favor of the alternative hypothesis. This suggests that the observed data is unlikely to occur if the null hypothesis is true, indicating that our assumption or forecasting model needs revision. On the other hand, if the p-value is above the significance level, we fail to reject the null hypothesis, indicating that our assumption or model is still valid.

Hypothesis testing provides a systematic and scientific approach to validate or reject assumptions about demand patterns. By employing this method in demand forecasting, Operations and Supply Chain Management professionals can ensure the accuracy and reliability of their forecasts, leading to more effective decision-making and improved supply chain performance.

In conclusion, hypothesis testing is a powerful tool in the field of demand forecasting. It allows us to assess the validity of assumptions and models, improving the accuracy of demand forecasts and ultimately optimizing operations and supply chain management. By embracing hypothesis testing, professionals in these niches can unlock the secrets behind demand forecasting and gain a competitive edge in the ever-evolving business landscape.

Chapter 5: Forecasting Accuracy and Evaluation

Measuring Forecast Accuracy

In the world of operations and supply chain management, forecasting plays a critical role in ensuring efficient production and distribution processes. Accurate forecasts enable businesses to make informed decisions, optimize inventory levels, and meet customer demands effectively. However, measuring forecast accuracy is essential to evaluate the reliability of these predictions and identify potential areas for improvement.

Forecast accuracy refers to the extent to which actual demand aligns with the forecasted values. It is crucial for organizations to determine the accuracy of their forecasts to assess the effectiveness of their forecasting models and techniques. By measuring forecast accuracy, businesses can gauge the impact of various factors such as seasonality, market trends, and external influences on the accuracy of their predictions.

There are several commonly used metrics to measure forecast accuracy. One widely used metric is Mean Absolute Percentage Error (MAPE), which calculates the average percentage difference between the forecasted and actual values. MAPE provides a standardized measure that can be used across different products or industries. Additionally, Mean Absolute Error (MAE) and Root Mean Squared Error (RMSE) are also popular metrics that measure the average and square root of the average difference between the forecasted and actual values, respectively.

Understanding these metrics is crucial for business professionals involved in operations and supply chain management. By comprehending the intricacies of measuring forecast accuracy, they can evaluate the performance of their forecasting models and make data-driven decisions to enhance their business operations.

Moreover, it is important to recognize that forecast accuracy is not a one-time evaluation but an ongoing process. Organizations must continuously monitor and measure forecast accuracy to identify patterns, trends, and potential biases in their forecasting models. Regular evaluation allows businesses to refine their forecasting techniques, incorporate new data sources, and adapt to changing market conditions.

In conclusion, measuring forecast accuracy is a crucial aspect of operations and supply chain management. It enables businesses to evaluate the reliability of their predictions, identify areas for improvement, and make informed decisions to optimize their production and distribution processes. By employing metrics such as MAPE, MAE, and RMSE, organizations can gauge the accuracy of their forecasts and continuously improve their forecasting models.

Mean Absolute Deviation (MAD)

In the realm of operations and supply chain management, accurate demand forecasting plays a critical role in optimizing inventory levels, production planning, and overall operational efficiency. One of the key metrics used to evaluate the accuracy of demand forecasts is the Mean Absolute Deviation (MAD). This subchapter will delve into the concept of MAD, its significance, and how it can be utilized to enhance demand forecasting.

MAD is a statistical measure that quantifies the average absolute difference between the forecasted demand and the actual demand. It provides a clear picture of the forecast's overall accuracy, regardless of whether the forecast overestimates or underestimates the actual demand. By focusing on the absolute values of the deviations, MAD eliminates any positive or negative bias, making it an unbiased and reliable measure for evaluating forecast accuracy.

For supply chain professionals and decision-makers, MAD offers valuable insights into the effectiveness of their demand forecasting models and processes. A lower MAD indicates a more accurate forecast, indicating that the organization is better equipped to meet customer demands while optimizing inventory levels and minimizing costs. Conversely, a higher MAD suggests a less accurate forecast, which can lead to excess inventory, stockouts, and increased costs.

To calculate MAD, the absolute value of the difference between the forecasted demand and the actual demand is calculated for each period, and then these absolute differences are averaged. The resulting value represents the average deviation of the forecast from the actual demand. By comparing this average deviation to the actual demand values, organizations can gauge the accuracy of their forecasts and identify areas for improvement.

MAD can be further utilized as a benchmarking tool to compare the accuracy of different forecasting models or techniques. By calculating MAD for multiple forecasting approaches, organizations can determine which model consistently provides the most accurate results and make informed decisions regarding the adoption or refinement of their forecasting methods.

In conclusion, MAD is an essential metric for evaluating the accuracy of demand forecasts in the field of operations and supply chain management. It provides an unbiased measure of forecast accuracy and helps organizations optimize inventory levels, production planning, and overall operational efficiency. By leveraging MAD, supply chain professionals can enhance their demand forecasting processes, minimize costs, and ultimately improve customer satisfaction.

Mean Absolute Percentage Error (MAPE)

In the world of demand forecasting, accuracy is key. The ability to predict future demand with precision can make or break a company's success. One widely used metric to evaluate the accuracy of forecasting models is the Mean Absolute Percentage Error (MAPE). This subchapter aims to demystify MAPE and explain its relevance to operations and supply chain management.

MAPE is a measure of forecast error expressed as a percentage. It provides insight into how accurate a forecasting model is by comparing the absolute difference between actual and forecasted values to the actual values themselves. The absolute difference is divided by the actual value and multiplied by 100 to obtain the percentage error. The average of these percentage errors across multiple data points gives the MAPE.

Why is MAPE important? Well, it allows businesses to assess the reliability of their forecasting models and make necessary adjustments. A lower MAPE indicates a more accurate forecasting model, while a higher MAPE suggests room for improvement. By monitoring and minimizing MAPE, companies can enhance their decision-making process, optimize inventory levels, and streamline their supply chain operations.

Operations and supply chain management professionals can benefit greatly from understanding MAPE. They rely heavily on demand forecasts to plan production, manage inventory, and allocate resources efficiently. By grasping the concept of MAPE, they can assess the accuracy of forecasts and make informed decisions to prevent stockouts or excessive inventory. This knowledge empowers them to optimize the supply chain, reduce costs, and enhance customer satisfaction.

While MAPE is a widely accepted error metric, it is important to note its limitations. MAPE tends to magnify small forecast errors when the actual values are close to zero. Additionally, it assumes that all data points are equally important, which may not always be the case. Therefore, it is recommended to use MAPE in conjunction with other error metrics to gain a comprehensive understanding of forecast accuracy.

In conclusion, MAPE plays a vital role in demand forecasting and holds significant value for professionals in operations and supply chain management. By understanding and monitoring MAPE, businesses can fine-tune their forecasting models, improve decision-making, and optimize their supply chain operations. With accurate demand forecasts, companies can stay ahead of the competition, reduce costs, and ultimately enhance customer satisfaction.

Tracking Signal

In the world of operations and supply chain management, tracking signal is a crucial concept that plays a significant role in demand forecasting. It serves as a powerful tool to evaluate the accuracy and reliability of a forecasting model. Whether you are a business professional, a student, or someone intrigued by the fascinating field of operations and supply chain management, understanding tracking signal can greatly enhance your knowledge and decision-making abilities.

At its core, tracking signal measures the difference between actual demand and forecasted demand over a specific period. It provides insights into the effectiveness of forecasting techniques and helps identify any biases or systematic errors in the forecasting process. By continuously monitoring and analyzing the tracking signal, businesses can adjust their forecasting models, ensure optimal inventory levels, and improve customer satisfaction.

One of the key benefits of tracking signal is its ability to detect and correct forecast errors before they lead to costly supply chain disruptions. By maintaining a low tracking signal value, businesses can minimize stockouts, reduce excess inventory, and streamline their operations. This not only saves costs but also improves overall customer experience, as products are readily available when needed.

Furthermore, tracking signal serves as an early warning system, alerting businesses to potential changes in demand patterns. By closely monitoring the signal, supply chain managers can proactively respond to shifts in customer preferences, market dynamics, or external factors such as economic conditions or natural disasters. This enables businesses to adapt their production and distribution strategies accordingly, ensuring maximum efficiency and agility.

To calculate the tracking signal, one typically divides the cumulative forecast error by the mean absolute deviation (MAD). A positive tracking signal indicates that the forecasts are consistently lower than actual demand, while a negative signal suggests consistently overestimating demand. By analyzing the direction and magnitude of the tracking signal, businesses can identify the specific areas where their forecasting models may need improvement.

In conclusion, tracking signal is an indispensable tool for operations and supply chain management professionals, providing valuable insights into the accuracy and reliability of demand forecasts. By continuously monitoring and analyzing the tracking signal, businesses can identify areas for improvement, make proactive adjustments, and optimize their inventory levels. With its ability to detect potential forecast errors and adapt to changing market conditions, tracking signal holds the key to effective demand forecasting, streamlined operations, and enhanced customer satisfaction.

Evaluating Forecasting Models

In the dynamic world of operations and supply chain management, accurate demand forecasting is crucial for businesses to succeed. However, with the multitude of forecasting models available, it can be challenging to determine which one is the most suitable and effective. This subchapter aims to provide a comprehensive overview of the various methods used to evaluate forecasting models, helping readers make informed decisions in their forecasting endeavors.

One of the most common evaluation techniques is measuring forecast error. This involves comparing the predicted values to the actual demand and calculating the difference between them. Several error measures exist, including mean absolute error (MAE), mean squared error (MSE), and root mean squared error (RMSE). These measures allow analysts to assess the level of accuracy achieved by a particular forecasting model.

Another widely used evaluation method is tracking forecast bias. Bias occurs when a forecasting model consistently overestimates or underestimates demand. Identifying and quantifying bias is important as it helps in understanding the systematic errors in a model's predictions. Common measures of bias include mean forecast error (MFE), mean percentage error (MPE), and mean absolute percentage error (MAPE).

An essential aspect of evaluating forecasting models is assessing their stability over time. A forecasting model should exhibit consistency in its performance, yielding reliable results across different time periods. Analyzing stability involves comparing the forecasting errors and bias over time to identify any patterns or changes that may affect the model's accuracy.

Furthermore, forecast accuracy can vary depending on the forecast horizon. Short-term forecasts, for example, are typically more accurate than long-term forecasts. Evaluating the performance of a model at different forecast horizons enables analysts to understand its strengths and limitations.

In addition to these quantitative evaluation techniques, it is crucial to consider the qualitative aspects of forecasting models. Factors such as ease of use, interpretability, and adaptability to changing circumstances should be taken into account. A forecasting model may be highly accurate, but if it is too complex to understand or implement, it may not be the most practical choice for a given business.

Ultimately, evaluating forecasting models requires a combination of quantitative analysis and qualitative judgment. It is essential to consider the specific needs and characteristics of the business, as well as the nature of the demand being forecasted. By carefully evaluating forecasting models, businesses can make informed decisions that lead to improved operational efficiency, reduced costs, and enhanced customer satisfaction.

Holdout Method

In the realm of demand forecasting, accuracy is key. Businesses rely on accurate demand forecasts to make informed decisions about production, inventory management, and overall supply chain efficiency. One popular method used to assess the accuracy of demand forecasting models is the Holdout Method.

The Holdout Method, also known as the validation set approach, is a technique used to evaluate the performance of a forecasting model. It involves splitting historical data into two subsets: a training set and a validation set. The training set is used to build the forecasting model, while the validation set is used to test the model's accuracy.

Why is the Holdout Method important in operations and supply chain management? Well, accuracy in demand forecasting directly impacts various aspects of these fields. By using the Holdout Method, businesses can assess the accuracy of their forecasting models and make necessary adjustments to improve their supply chain operations.

The process begins by selecting a representative historical dataset. This dataset is then divided into a training set, which typically comprises 70-80% of the data, and a validation set, which makes up the remaining 20-30%. The training set is used to develop the forecasting model, whether it be a statistical model, machine learning algorithm, or a combination of both.

Once the model is built using the training set, it is applied to the validation set to generate forecasts. These forecasts are then compared to the actual demand values from the validation set. The accuracy of the model is evaluated using various statistical measures, such as mean absolute percentage error (MAPE) or root mean squared error (RMSE).

By comparing the forecasted values to the actual demand values, businesses can determine the accuracy of their forecasting models. If the forecasts closely align with the actual demand, the model is considered accurate and reliable. However, if there are significant discrepancies, adjustments need to be made to improve the forecasting model's performance.

The Holdout Method allows businesses to identify any biases or errors in their forecasting models. It helps them understand the model's limitations and areas for improvement. By fine-tuning the model based on the performance evaluation from the validation set, businesses can enhance their demand forecasting accuracy and optimize their operations and supply chains accordingly.

In conclusion, the Holdout Method is a valuable technique in demand forecasting that allows businesses to assess the accuracy of their forecasting models. It helps them identify any discrepancies between the forecasted values and the actual demand, allowing for adjustments and improvements. By utilizing this method, businesses can enhance their operations and supply chain management, leading to increased efficiency and profitability.

Cross-Validation Technique

In the realm of operations and supply chain management, accurate demand forecasting is crucial for businesses to effectively plan their production, inventory, and logistics processes. One of the most powerful tools for achieving reliable forecasts is the cross-validation technique. This subchapter aims to demystify this technique, breaking it down into simple terms for everyone to understand.

Cross-validation is a method used to assess the performance of a forecasting model by testing its accuracy on unseen data. It involves dividing the available historical data into multiple subsets or folds. The model is trained on a portion of the data, and then its ability to predict the remaining data is evaluated. This process is repeated several times, each time using a different subset for testing and the rest for training. By comparing the predicted values with the actual values, the accuracy of the model can be determined.

Why is cross-validation important? Well, traditional methods of assessing a model's performance, such as comparing its predictions with the same data it was trained on, can be misleading. This is because the model may simply have memorized the patterns in the training data without truly understanding the underlying relationships. Cross-validation helps address this issue by testing the model on unseen data, providing a more reliable estimate of its predictive capabilities.

There are various cross-validation techniques, including k-fold cross-validation, leave-one-out cross-validation, and stratified cross-validation. Each technique has its own advantages and is suitable for different scenarios. For instance, k-fold cross-validation is often preferred when the dataset is large, while leave-one-out cross-validation is more appropriate when the dataset is small.

By employing cross-validation, businesses can select the most accurate forecasting model for their operations and supply chain management. This technique allows for a comprehensive evaluation of different models, enabling informed decision-making. Moreover, cross-validation can also help identify any potential overfitting issues, where a model performs exceedingly well on the training data but fails to generalize to new data.

In conclusion, the cross-validation technique is a powerful tool in the field of demand forecasting. It provides a robust and objective assessment of forecasting models, allowing businesses to make informed decisions about their operations and supply chain management strategies. By utilizing this technique, organizations can enhance their forecasting accuracy, optimize their resources, and ultimately improve customer satisfaction.

Forecast Error Decomposition

Forecasting is an essential aspect of operations and supply chain management. It helps businesses make informed decisions about production, inventory, and customer demand. However, no forecasting method is perfect, and errors are bound to occur. Understanding these errors and their sources is crucial for improving the accuracy of future forecasts. This subchapter delves into the concept of forecast error decomposition, providing a layman's perspective on this vital topic.

Forecast error decomposition is a technique used to break down the error in a forecast into its various components. By identifying and analyzing these components, businesses can gain valuable insights into the factors influencing forecast accuracy. This knowledge enables them to take corrective actions and refine their forecasting techniques.

The two primary components of forecast error decomposition are bias and random error. Bias refers to a consistent overestimation or underestimation of demand over time. It can be caused by factors such as inaccurate historical data, changing market conditions, or biased judgment. Random error, on the other hand, is the unpredictable variation that occurs in every forecast. It can be influenced by factors such as unexpected events, human error, or limitations in the forecasting model.

By decomposing forecast errors into bias and random error components, businesses can identify the sources of inaccuracy. This knowledge allows them to make targeted improvements in their forecasting process. For example, if bias is consistently present, businesses can adjust their forecasting model or collect more accurate historical data to reduce the bias. If random error is the primary source of forecast inaccuracy, businesses can focus on improving the statistical techniques used in their forecasting models.

Furthermore, forecast error decomposition can also help businesses evaluate the impact of specific events or factors on forecast accuracy. By comparing forecast errors before and after a significant event, businesses can determine the extent to which the event influenced the forecast. This information can guide decision-making, such as adjusting production levels or inventory management in response to future similar events.

In conclusion, forecast error decomposition is a powerful tool for analyzing and improving forecast accuracy in operations and supply chain management. By breaking down forecast errors into bias and random error components, businesses can identify the sources of inaccuracy and take appropriate corrective actions. This knowledge enables businesses to make more informed decisions, optimize production, and improve customer satisfaction.

Chapter 6: Improving Forecasting Accuracy

Demand Sensing and Shaping

In today's fast-paced and dynamic business environment, accurate demand forecasting is crucial for the success of any organization. However, traditional demand forecasting methods often fall short in capturing the rapidly changing consumer behavior and market trends. This is where demand sensing and shaping comes into play, revolutionizing the field of operations and supply chain management.

Demand sensing involves the real-time monitoring and analysis of various data sources to detect changes in customer demand patterns. By leveraging advanced technologies such as artificial intelligence, machine learning, and big data analytics, organizations can gain valuable insights into customer behavior, market trends, and supply chain dynamics. This real-time information enables businesses to make informed decisions and respond swiftly to fluctuations in demand.

Furthermore, demand shaping goes beyond simply predicting future demand. It involves actively influencing and shaping customer demand through various strategies and initiatives. By understanding customer preferences, segmenting the market, and tailoring product offerings accordingly, organizations can create a demand-driven supply chain that maximizes customer satisfaction while minimizing costs.

One of the key benefits of demand sensing and shaping is improved inventory management. By accurately sensing customer demand and shaping it through targeted marketing efforts, organizations can optimize their inventory levels. This leads to reduced stockouts, lower carrying costs, and improved profitability. Additionally, demand sensing and shaping help in reducing lead times, enhancing customer service levels, and fostering collaboration between different stakeholders in the supply chain.

Moreover, demand sensing and shaping also enable organizations to capitalize on emerging trends and opportunities. By closely monitoring social media, online reviews, and market research data, businesses can identify new customer preferences and tailor their products or services to meet these evolving demands. This proactive approach ensures that companies stay ahead of the competition and remain relevant in the ever-changing marketplace.

In conclusion, demand sensing and shaping are critical components of modern operations and supply chain management. By harnessing the power of real-time data analysis and leveraging innovative technologies, organizations can accurately sense customer demand, shape it through targeted strategies, and drive business growth. Embracing demand sensing and shaping not only improves inventory management and customer service but also allows businesses to stay agile and responsive in an increasingly competitive landscape.

Collaborative Forecasting

In the realm of operations and supply chain management, accurate demand forecasting is the cornerstone of success. It allows businesses to optimize their inventory, plan production, and ensure customer satisfaction. However, traditional forecasting methods often fall short in capturing the intricacies of a dynamic market. This is where collaborative forecasting comes into play.

Collaborative forecasting is a revolutionary approach that leverages the collective intelligence and expertise of various stakeholders within a supply chain. By involving key players such as suppliers, distributors, retailers, and even customers, businesses can tap into a wealth of knowledge and insights that go beyond the limitations of traditional forecasting techniques.

One of the primary benefits of collaborative forecasting is the enhanced accuracy it offers. By incorporating the input of multiple stakeholders, businesses can capture a broader range of perspectives and factors that impact demand. This collaborative approach reduces the likelihood of biases or blind spots that may arise from relying solely on internal data or predictions. With a more accurate demand forecast, businesses can optimize their inventory levels, minimize stockouts, and reduce carrying costs.

Furthermore, collaborative forecasting fosters better communication and coordination throughout the supply chain. By involving all relevant parties in the forecasting process, businesses can align their plans, share information, and identify potential bottlenecks or constraints. This holistic approach enhances transparency and allows for proactive decision-making, leading to improved operational efficiency and reduced lead times.

Collaborative forecasting also enhances customer satisfaction. By involving customers in the forecasting process, businesses can gain valuable insights into their preferences, buying behavior, and future demand patterns. This customer-centric approach enables businesses to tailor their production, marketing, and inventory strategies accordingly, thus meeting customer expectations more effectively and reducing the risk of overstocks or understocks.

Implementing collaborative forecasting, however, requires a shift in mindset and a willingness to embrace a more inclusive and participatory approach. It calls for the adoption of advanced technologies, such as cloud-based platforms or collaborative software, to facilitate seamless information sharing and collaboration among stakeholders.

In conclusion, collaborative forecasting is a game-changer in the field of demand forecasting and supply chain management. By harnessing the power of collective intelligence and involving key stakeholders, businesses can achieve more accurate forecasts, improved operational efficiency, and enhanced customer satisfaction. Embracing this collaborative approach can help businesses stay ahead in an increasingly competitive market landscape.

Incorporating External Factors

In the realm of operations and supply chain management, it is crucial to understand that demand forecasting cannot be solely based on internal factors. To accurately predict future demand, one must also take into account the various external factors that can significantly influence consumer behavior and market conditions. This subchapter delves into the importance of incorporating these external factors into the demand forecasting process and how they can enhance the accuracy and reliability of predictions.

External factors encompass a wide range of variables, including economic indicators, competitive landscape, technological advancements, cultural shifts, and even natural disasters. These factors have the potential to impact consumer preferences, purchasing power, and overall market dynamics. Ignoring or overlooking these factors can lead to flawed forecasts, resulting in overstocking or understocking of inventory, inefficient production planning, and missed sales opportunities.

One of the key external factors to consider is the state of the economy. Economic indicators such as GDP growth rates, inflation, interest rates, and employment levels can greatly influence consumer spending habits. During periods of economic downturn, consumers tend to tighten their belts and reduce discretionary spending, leading to a decline in demand for non-essential goods and services. Conversely, during economic upswings, consumers often exhibit increased confidence and willingness to spend, driving up demand.

Competitive analysis is another critical external factor to consider. Monitoring and understanding the strategies of competitors can provide valuable insights into market dynamics and potential demand fluctuations. Changes in pricing, promotional activities, new product launches, or shifts in market share can all impact the demand for a particular product or service.

Technological advancements are also significant external factors to incorporate. The introduction of new technologies can disrupt existing markets, change consumer preferences, and create new demand patterns. For example, the rise of e-commerce has revolutionized the retail industry, altering consumer buying behavior and demand for traditional brick-and-mortar stores.

Cultural shifts and social trends are external factors that can influence demand forecasting. Changes in social norms, cultural values, and lifestyle preferences can impact the demand for specific products or services. For instance, the growing trend towards sustainability and eco-consciousness has led to an increased demand for environmentally friendly products.

Natural disasters and extreme weather events are external factors that can have a profound impact on demand forecasting. These events can disrupt supply chains, cause shortages or price spikes, and alter consumer behavior. For example, a hurricane may lead to increased demand for certain goods such as bottled water, batteries, and emergency supplies.

Incorporating external factors into the demand forecasting process requires a comprehensive and data-driven approach. By analyzing historical data, conducting market research, and staying informed about the latest trends, organizations can gain a deeper understanding of the external factors that shape demand. This knowledge allows for more accurate demand forecasts, enabling businesses to optimize their operations, enhance customer satisfaction, and effectively manage their supply chains.

Machine Learning in Demand Forecasting

In today's dynamic and ever-changing business landscape, accurate demand forecasting is crucial for companies to optimize their operations and supply chain management. With the advent of machine learning, demand forecasting has been revolutionized, offering businesses unparalleled insights and predictive capabilities.

Machine learning algorithms have the ability to analyze vast amounts of historical data and identify patterns that may not be immediately apparent to human analysts. By leveraging this technology, companies can make more informed decisions and minimize the risk of stockouts or excess inventory. This subchapter will delve into the key concepts of machine learning in demand forecasting, providing a layman's perspective for readers from all backgrounds.

One of the primary advantages of machine learning in demand forecasting is its ability to handle complex data sets. Traditional forecasting methods often struggle to capture the intricate relationships between various factors that influence demand, such as seasonality, promotions, competitor activities, and economic trends. Machine learning algorithms, on the other hand, can identify these complex patterns and make accurate predictions based on historical data and real-time information.

Another benefit of machine learning in demand forecasting is its adaptability. These algorithms can continuously learn and improve their forecasting accuracy as new data becomes available. By automatically adjusting their models and incorporating the latest information, machine learning algorithms can provide businesses with up-to-date and reliable demand forecasts.

Furthermore, machine learning algorithms can also incorporate external data sources, such as social media sentiment, weather forecasts, or economic indicators, to enhance the accuracy of demand forecasts. By considering these external factors, businesses gain a holistic view of the market and can respond quickly to changing consumer preferences or market conditions.

It is important to note that while machine learning algorithms offer significant advantages in demand forecasting, they are not a silver bullet. They require careful selection and customization to suit the specific needs of each business. Moreover, human expertise is essential in interpreting the results, validating the forecasts, and making informed decisions based on the algorithm's output.

In conclusion, machine learning has revolutionized the field of demand forecasting, enabling businesses to make more accurate predictions and optimize their operations and supply chain management. By leveraging the power of machine learning algorithms, companies can gain a competitive edge by minimizing costs, improving customer satisfaction, and maximizing profitability. However, it is crucial for businesses to combine the capabilities of machine learning with human expertise to ensure the best outcomes.

Chapter 7: Case Studies

Retail Industry

The retail industry is an ever-evolving and dynamic sector that plays a crucial role in our daily lives. From the local corner store to giant multinational chains, the retail industry spans across various sectors, including food and beverages, clothing, electronics, and more. Understanding the intricacies of the retail industry is essential for anyone interested in operations and supply chain management.

In this subchapter of "The Science Behind Demand Forecasting: A Layman's Perspective," we will delve into the fascinating world of the retail industry. We will explore the key players, challenges, and trends that shape this sector and how they relate to demand forecasting.

To begin with, let's discuss the key players in the retail industry. Retailers can be classified into different categories based on their business model. These may include brick-and-mortar stores, e-commerce platforms, and omnichannel retailers that combine both physical and online presence. Each category has its own set of challenges and opportunities when it comes to demand forecasting, as the behavior of consumers can vary significantly across these channels.

Next, we will examine the challenges faced by retailers in demand forecasting. Factors such as changing consumer preferences, seasonality, and fluctuations in the economy can pose significant challenges in accurately predicting demand. Moreover, the rise of e-commerce and the increasing competition among retailers have further intensified the need for efficient forecasting techniques.

Furthermore, this subchapter will shed light on the latest trends in the retail industry that impact demand forecasting. For instance, the integration of technology, such as artificial intelligence and machine learning, has revolutionized the way retailers forecast demand. These advanced techniques enable retailers to analyze vast amounts of data and make more accurate predictions, ultimately leading to better inventory management and customer satisfaction.

The subchapter will also touch upon the importance of collaboration and communication between retailers and their suppliers. Effective supply chain management is crucial in ensuring the availability of products at the right time and in the right quantity. By establishing strong relationships and sharing information, retailers can enhance their forecasting accuracy and streamline their operations.

In conclusion, the retail industry is a complex and vibrant sector that presents both opportunities and challenges for demand forecasting. Understanding the intricacies of this industry is essential for individuals interested in operations and supply chain management. By exploring the key players, challenges, and trends in the retail industry, this subchapter aims to provide valuable insights that can help readers optimize their demand forecasting techniques and drive success in the retail sector.

Manufacturing Industry

The manufacturing industry plays a vital role in the global economy, serving as the backbone of various sectors such as automotive, electronics, pharmaceuticals, and consumer goods. It encompasses a wide range of activities involved in transforming raw materials into finished products ready for consumption or further processing. Understanding the workings of the manufacturing industry is crucial for individuals interested in operations and supply chain management.

One of the key aspects of the manufacturing industry is efficiency. Manufacturers strive to optimize their production processes to minimize waste, reduce costs, and improve overall productivity. This involves carefully managing resources, including labor, materials, and machinery, to ensure smooth operations. By implementing lean manufacturing principles and embracing emerging technologies, such as automation and robotics, manufacturers can streamline their operations and achieve higher levels of efficiency.

Another critical factor in the manufacturing industry is quality control. Manufacturers are responsible for ensuring that their products meet or exceed customer expectations. This involves implementing stringent quality control measures throughout the production process, from raw material inspection to final product testing. By maintaining high-quality standards, manufacturers can build trust with customers, enhance brand reputation, and gain a competitive edge in the market.

In today's globalized world, the manufacturing industry faces numerous challenges, including supply chain disruptions, changing consumer demands, and rapidly evolving technologies. As a result, manufacturers must embrace innovation and adapt to these changes to remain competitive. This includes leveraging advanced technologies, such as internet of things (IoT) devices and data analytics, to improve inventory management, forecast demand more accurately, and enhance overall operational efficiency.

Moreover, sustainability has become a key focus for the manufacturing industry. Manufacturers are increasingly adopting environmentally friendly practices and pursuing sustainable manufacturing methods to minimize their carbon footprint. This includes using renewable energy sources, reducing waste generation, and implementing recycling programs. By embracing sustainability, manufacturers not only contribute to environmental preservation but also enhance their brand image and appeal to environmentally conscious consumers.

In conclusion, the manufacturing industry is a dynamic and essential component of the global economy. Its efficient operations, emphasis on quality control, ability to adapt to changing market conditions, and commitment to sustainability make it a fascinating field to explore for individuals interested in operations and supply chain management. By understanding the intricacies of the manufacturing industry, professionals can make informed decisions and contribute to the success of their organizations.

Service Industry

The service industry plays a vital role in our modern economy, providing intangible products and experiences that cater to the needs and desires of consumers. From restaurants and hotels to healthcare providers and financial institutions, the service industry encompasses a wide range of businesses that aim to deliver exceptional customer experiences. In this subchapter, we will explore the intricacies of the service industry, its challenges, and the importance of demand forecasting in operations and supply chain management.

Unlike the manufacturing industry, where tangible goods are produced, the service industry focuses on delivering intangible services that cannot be physically measured or stored. This unique characteristic poses a significant challenge in accurately predicting and managing demand. However, with the advent of advanced technologies and data analytics, demand forecasting has become a crucial tool for service industry professionals.

In the service industry, demand forecasting involves predicting consumer behavior and anticipating their needs to ensure optimal resource allocation. Whether it's determining the number of staff required during peak hours at a restaurant or forecasting patient visits at a healthcare facility, accurate demand forecasting allows service providers to optimize their operations and deliver the best possible service to their customers.

One of the key reasons why demand forecasting is essential in the service industry is its direct impact on customer satisfaction. By accurately predicting demand, service providers can avoid long waiting times, ensure adequate staffing levels, and maintain high service quality. This, in turn, leads to better customer experiences, increased loyalty, and positive word-of-mouth recommendations.

Moreover, demand forecasting also helps service industry businesses manage their inventory and supply chain more efficiently. By accurately predicting demand, companies can avoid overstocking or understocking inventory, reducing costs and maximizing profitability. Additionally, demand forecasting enables service providers to plan their procurement and supply chain activities effectively, ensuring the availability of necessary resources to meet customer demand.

In conclusion, the service industry is a crucial sector of the economy, providing intangible services that cater to consumer needs. Demand forecasting plays a critical role in operations and supply chain management within the service industry, allowing businesses to accurately predict customer demand, optimize resource allocation, and enhance customer satisfaction. By leveraging advanced technologies and data analytics, service industry professionals can overcome the unique challenges associated with intangible services and achieve operational excellence.

Chapter 8: Future Trends in Demand Forecasting

Artificial Intelligence and Predictive Analytics

In recent years, the fields of Operations and Supply Chain Management have witnessed a significant transformation due to the integration of Artificial Intelligence (AI) and Predictive Analytics. This subchapter aims to provide a layman's perspective on these groundbreaking technologies and their impact on demand forecasting.

Artificial Intelligence, a term often associated with science fiction, has become a reality in today's digital age. It refers to machines that are programmed to mimic human intelligence and perform tasks that would typically require human intelligence. When applied to demand forecasting, AI algorithms analyze vast amounts of historical data, identify patterns, and make accurate predictions about future demand patterns.

Predictive Analytics, on the other hand, is the practice of extracting information from existing data sets to determine patterns and predict future outcomes. By utilizing statistical algorithms and machine learning techniques, predictive analytics enables businesses to identify trends, uncover hidden insights, and make informed decisions based on data-driven forecasts.

The integration of AI and Predictive Analytics in demand forecasting has revolutionized the way businesses operate. Traditional forecasting methods heavily relied on historical data and manual analysis, which often led to inaccurate predictions. However, with AI and Predictive Analytics, organizations can now leverage real-time data, market trends, customer preferences, and external factors to generate more precise demand forecasts.

One of the key advantages of AI and Predictive Analytics in demand forecasting is their ability to handle complex and dynamic data sets. These technologies can process large volumes of structured and unstructured data, including social media feeds, customer reviews, and market trends, to gain a holistic understanding of demand drivers. By analyzing this comprehensive data, businesses can make more accurate predictions, optimize inventory levels, and ensure efficient supply chain management.

Furthermore, AI and Predictive Analytics enhance the responsiveness of businesses to changing market dynamics. Demand patterns are constantly evolving, and businesses need to adapt quickly to meet customer expectations. With AI algorithms continuously learning and improving their predictions, businesses can proactively respond to market shifts, reduce stockouts, and minimize excess inventory.

In conclusion, the integration of Artificial Intelligence and Predictive Analytics has transformed demand forecasting in the fields of Operations and Supply Chain Management. These technologies empower businesses with accurate predictions, optimize inventory management, and improve overall supply chain efficiency. Whether you are a business owner, supply chain professional, or simply interested in the topic, understanding the science behind AI and Predictive Analytics is crucial for staying ahead in today's dynamic market.

Big Data and Demand Forecasting

In recent years, the world has witnessed an explosion of data generation and collection from various sources. This massive amount of information, known as Big Data, has the potential to revolutionize the way businesses operate, particularly in the realm of demand forecasting. In this subchapter, we will explore the intersection of Big Data and demand forecasting, shedding light on how this powerful combination is changing the game for operations and supply chain management.

Traditionally, demand forecasting relied on historical sales data, market trends, and the expertise of industry professionals. While these methods have proven effective to some extent, they often fall short in capturing the complexity and volatility of today's markets. This is where Big Data comes into play. With access to vast amounts of real-time data from a wide range of sources, businesses can now gain deeper insights into consumer behavior, market dynamics, and emerging trends.

One of the key advantages of Big Data in demand forecasting is its ability to capture and analyze unstructured data. Social media platforms, online forums, and customer reviews provide valuable insights into consumer sentiments and preferences. By leveraging sentiment analysis algorithms and natural language processing techniques, businesses can tap into this wealth of unstructured data to gain a more accurate understanding of customer demand.

Another significant benefit of Big Data is its ability to incorporate external factors that impact demand. Weather patterns, economic indicators, and competitor activities are just a few examples of external variables that can influence consumer behavior. By integrating these factors into demand forecasting models, businesses can enhance the accuracy of their predictions and make more informed decisions.

However, it is important to note that Big Data is not a magic bullet. The sheer volume and complexity of data can be overwhelming, making it challenging to extract meaningful insights. Therefore, businesses need to invest in advanced analytics tools and technologies to effectively process and interpret Big Data. Additionally, data privacy and security concerns must be addressed to ensure the ethical and responsible use of customer information.

In conclusion, the marriage of Big Data and demand forecasting holds immense potential for operations and supply chain management. By harnessing the power of Big Data analytics, businesses can improve the accuracy of their demand forecasts, anticipate market trends, and optimize their supply chain operations. However, it is crucial for businesses to invest in the right resources and strategies to effectively leverage Big Data and ensure its ethical use. With the right approach, Big Data can truly revolutionize the way businesses forecast and meet customer demand in today's dynamic and ever-evolving markets.

Internet of Things (IoT) and Demand Forecasting

In recent years, the Internet of Things (IoT) has emerged as a revolutionary technology that is transforming industries across the globe. From healthcare to manufacturing, IoT is playing a vital role in streamlining processes, improving efficiency, and enhancing productivity. One area where IoT is making a significant impact is demand forecasting, particularly in the realm of operations and supply chain management.

Demand forecasting is a critical aspect of any business, as it helps organizations predict customer demand accurately and plan their production and supply chain activities accordingly. Traditionally, demand forecasting relied on historical data, market research, and statistical models. However, with the advent of IoT, businesses now have access to real-time data from a myriad of sources, enabling them to make more informed and accurate forecasts.

IoT devices, such as sensors and smart devices, are capable of capturing and transmitting vast amounts of data, providing valuable insights into various aspects of the supply chain. For instance, sensors placed on production lines can monitor the performance of machinery and identify potential breakdowns or maintenance needs in real-time. By integrating this data with demand forecasting models, organizations can accurately predict the impact of such disruptions on production and plan accordingly.

Furthermore, IoT devices can be deployed at various touchpoints in the supply chain, including warehouses, distribution centers, and retail stores. These devices can track inventory levels, monitor product movement, and collect data on customer behavior. By analyzing this data, organizations can identify patterns and trends, enabling them to make more accurate demand forecasts and optimize their supply chain processes.

Moreover, IoT-powered demand forecasting can also enable businesses to adopt a more proactive approach to inventory management. By constantly monitoring inventory levels and demand patterns, organizations can identify potential stockouts or overstock situations in advance. This allows them to take timely actions, such as adjusting production schedules or initiating procurement activities, to avoid disruptions and optimize inventory levels.

In conclusion, the integration of IoT technology with demand forecasting has revolutionized operations and supply chain management. Real-time data from IoT devices provides organizations with valuable insights into production, inventory, and customer behavior, enabling them to make more accurate demand forecasts. By leveraging this technology, businesses can optimize their supply chain processes, improve efficiency, and ultimately enhance customer satisfaction. The future of demand forecasting lies in embracing IoT and harnessing its power to drive innovation and success in the ever-evolving world of operations and supply chain management.

Chapter 9: Practical Applications and Tips

Implementing Demand Forecasting Systems

Demand forecasting is a crucial aspect of operations and supply chain management. It helps organizations predict future demand for their products or services, enabling them to make informed decisions regarding production, inventory management, and resource allocation. Implementing effective demand forecasting systems can significantly enhance operational efficiency and minimize costs while maximizing customer satisfaction.

This subchapter delves into the various aspects of implementing demand forecasting systems and offers valuable insights for individuals interested in operations and supply chain management.

1. Understanding the Need for Demand Forecasting Systems: To begin with, it is crucial to comprehend the importance of demand forecasting in the overall business strategy. This section provides an overview of how demand forecasting systems can optimize production, streamline inventory management processes, and reduce the risk of stockouts or excess inventory.

2. Selecting the Right Demand Forecasting System: Choosing the appropriate demand forecasting system is essential for accurate predictions. This section explores different types of forecasting methods, including qualitative, quantitative, and hybrid approaches. It also discusses the factors to consider when selecting a demand forecasting system, such as data availability, industry-specific requirements, and the organization's goals.

3. Data Collection and Analysis: Accurate demand forecasting relies on comprehensive data collection and analysis. This section covers the importance of data quality, sources of data, and the necessary tools and techniques for data analysis. It also emphasizes the significance of historical data, market trends, and external factors in demand forecasting.

4. Implementing Demand Forecasting Software: Implementing demand forecasting software can significantly simplify the forecasting process. This section provides an overview of different software options available in the market and highlights the features to consider when choosing a suitable solution. It also offers tips on successfully integrating the software into existing systems and training employees to utilize the software effectively.

5. Evaluating and Improving Demand Forecasting Systems: Demand forecasting is an ongoing process that requires continuous evaluation and improvement. This section discusses the importance of monitoring forecasting accuracy, identifying and addressing forecasting errors, and incorporating feedback from customers and stakeholders. It also explores the role of analytics and machine learning in enhancing demand forecasting accuracy.

By implementing robust demand forecasting systems, organizations can optimize their operations, reduce costs, and deliver exceptional customer experiences. This subchapter provides a comprehensive guide to help individuals in operations and supply chain management understand and implement effective demand forecasting systems, ensuring their organizations stay ahead in a dynamic and competitive business environment.

Best Practices for Demand Forecasting

Demand forecasting is a crucial aspect of operations and supply chain management. It enables businesses to make informed decisions regarding production, inventory management, and overall business strategy. However, accurate demand forecasting can be challenging, especially in today's dynamic and uncertain market conditions. To address this challenge, businesses must adopt best practices for demand forecasting. This subchapter explores some of these best practices and provides valuable insights for professionals in operations and supply chain management.

1. Data-driven Approach: Demand forecasting should be based on reliable and relevant data. Collecting historical sales data, customer feedback, market trends, and industry reports can help businesses gain insights into future demand patterns. Leveraging advanced analytics and machine learning algorithms can further enhance the accuracy of forecasts.

2. Collaborative Forecasting: Involving key stakeholders such as sales representatives, marketing teams, and customers in the forecasting process can lead to more accurate predictions. Their insights and expertise can provide a more comprehensive understanding of market dynamics, customer behavior, and emerging trends.

3. Continuous Monitoring and Updating: Demand forecasting is not a one-time activity. It requires continuous monitoring and updating to reflect changing market conditions. Regularly reviewing and adjusting forecasts based on real-time data and feedback can help businesses stay agile and responsive to market fluctuations.

4. Incorporating External Factors: Demand forecasts should not solely rely on internal data. External factors like economic conditions, political events, weather patterns, and competitor activities can significantly impact demand. Integrating these external factors into the forecasting models can improve accuracy and enable proactive decision-making.

5. Scenario Planning: Considering multiple scenarios can enhance the robustness of demand forecasts. By analyzing best-case, worst-case, and most likely scenarios, businesses can better prepare for various outcomes and mitigate potential risks. This approach enables them to develop contingency plans and optimize resource allocation.

6. Regular Forecast Accuracy Evaluation: Assessing the accuracy of past forecasts is crucial for continuous improvement. By comparing actual sales data with projected forecasts, businesses can identify areas of improvement, refine forecasting models, and enhance overall accuracy over time.

By adopting these best practices for demand forecasting, businesses can optimize their operations, reduce costs, minimize inventory holding, and enhance customer satisfaction. Furthermore, accurate demand forecasting enables businesses to align their supply chain activities with market demand, resulting in improved efficiency and competitiveness.

In conclusion, demand forecasting is a critical component of operations and supply chain management. By following best practices such as data-driven approaches, collaboration, continuous monitoring, and scenario planning, businesses can enhance the accuracy of their forecasts and make informed decisions. Implementing these practices will not only optimize operations but also contribute to overall business success in today's dynamic marketplace.

also contribute to overall business success in today's dynamic marketplace.

Overcoming Challenges in Demand Forecasting

Introduction:

In the ever-changing world of operations and supply chain management, accurate demand forecasting is crucial to success. It allows companies to optimize their inventory levels, plan production efficiently, and ultimately meet customer expectations. However, demand forecasting is not without its challenges. In this subchapter, we will explore some of the common obstacles faced in demand forecasting and discuss strategies to overcome them.

1. Volatile Market Dynamics:

One of the primary challenges in demand forecasting is dealing with volatile market dynamics. Rapid shifts in consumer preferences, economic conditions, and technological advancements can significantly impact demand patterns. To overcome this challenge, companies should adopt agile forecasting techniques that provide real-time data and employ advanced analytics. By continuously monitoring market trends, companies can adjust their forecasts promptly and make more informed decisions.

2. Data Inaccuracy:

Another significant challenge in demand forecasting lies in the accuracy of the data used. Data collection, storage, and analysis processes can introduce errors, leading to inaccurate forecasts. To address this, companies should invest in robust data management systems that ensure data integrity and reliability. Regular data cleansing and validation procedures should be implemented to eliminate any inaccuracies. Moreover, companies can leverage machine learning algorithms to identify and correct anomalies in the data, improving the forecasting accuracy.

3. Seasonality and Trends:

Seasonality and trends pose unique challenges to demand forecasting. Predicting demand during peak seasons or identifying emerging trends accurately can be difficult. To overcome this, companies should analyze historical data to identify patterns and incorporate them into their forecasting models. Collaborating with sales and marketing teams can also provide valuable insights into upcoming promotions, new product launches, or seasonal fluctuations.

4. Supply Chain Disruptions:

Supply chain disruptions, such as natural disasters, political unrest, or global crises, can greatly impact demand forecasting. These unforeseen events can disrupt the availability of raw materials, transportation systems, and manufacturing processes. To mitigate the impact of such disruptions, companies should maintain robust risk management strategies. Diversifying suppliers, implementing contingency plans, and utilizing predictive analytics can help anticipate and react to potential disruptions effectively.

Conclusion:

Demand forecasting is a complex task, but by understanding and addressing the challenges it poses, companies can improve their operational efficiency and customer satisfaction. By embracing advanced technologies, investing in accurate data management, and adopting agile forecasting techniques, organizations can overcome the hurdles in demand forecasting and make more informed decisions. In the dynamic world of operations and supply chain management, staying ahead of the curve is essential, and overcoming these challenges is a crucial step in achieving success.

Chapter 10: Conclusion

Summarizing Key Concepts

In this subchapter, we will delve into the fundamental concepts of demand forecasting and provide a concise summary of the key ideas discussed throughout this book. Whether you are an operations manager, a supply chain professional, or simply curious about the science behind demand forecasting, this summary will help you grasp the essential aspects of this important field.

Demand forecasting is the process of predicting future customer demand based on historical data, market trends, and other relevant factors. By accurately forecasting demand, businesses can optimize their production, inventory management, and overall supply chain operations. This subchapter aims to demystify the science behind demand forecasting and present it in a layman's perspective.

Firstly, we explore the importance of demand forecasting and its impact on various aspects of an organization. From inventory control to capacity planning, demand forecasting serves as a critical tool for decision-making. We discuss how accurate forecasting can lead to cost savings, improved customer satisfaction, and enhanced overall operational efficiency.

Next, we introduce different demand forecasting techniques. These include qualitative methods, such as expert opinion and market research, as well as quantitative methods, such as time series analysis and causal modeling. By understanding the strengths and limitations of each technique, you can choose the most suitable approach for your specific forecasting needs.

We also emphasize the significance of data in demand forecasting. High-quality and relevant data are essential for accurate forecasting. We discuss the importance of data collection, data cleansing, and data analysis techniques to ensure the reliability of your forecasts. Additionally, we touch upon the role of technology and software solutions in automating the forecasting process and handling large datasets.

Throughout this subchapter, we stress the need for continuous improvement in demand forecasting. Markets are dynamic, and demand patterns can change rapidly. By monitoring and evaluating the accuracy of your forecasts, you can identify areas for improvement and make necessary adjustments to your forecasting models.

In summary, demand forecasting is a vital aspect of operations and supply chain management. It enables businesses to optimize their resources, reduce costs, and meet customer demands effectively. By understanding the key concepts presented in this subchapter, you will gain a solid foundation in demand forecasting and be better equipped to make informed decisions in your professional endeavors.

Importance of Demand Forecasting in Decision Making

Subchapter: Importance of Demand Forecasting in Decision Making

In today's fast-paced and dynamic business environment, accurate and reliable decision-making is of utmost importance for organizations across all industries. One critical aspect that plays a significant role in this process is demand forecasting. Demand forecasting is the practice of estimating the demand for a product or service in the future, based on historical data, market trends, and other relevant factors. It serves as the backbone of effective decision-making, particularly in the field of operations and supply chain management.

For companies operating in the operations and supply chain management niches, demand forecasting serves multiple purposes. Firstly, it provides insights into future demand patterns, allowing organizations to align their production, procurement, and inventory management strategies accordingly. By accurately forecasting demand, businesses can optimize their resources, minimize wastage, and reduce costs. This leads to improved operational efficiency and customer satisfaction.

Secondly, demand forecasting helps organizations make informed decisions regarding capacity planning and expansion. By anticipating future demand, companies can gauge the need for additional production facilities, warehouse space, or transportation infrastructure. This proactive approach ensures that organizations are adequately prepared to meet customer demands and avoid potential bottlenecks or supply chain disruptions.

Furthermore, demand forecasting enables effective inventory management. By understanding future demand patterns, businesses can determine optimal inventory levels, reducing the risk of overstocking or stockouts. Maintaining the right stock levels ensures that products are readily available to customers, thereby enhancing customer loyalty and preventing lost sales opportunities.

In addition to operational benefits, demand forecasting also plays a vital role in strategic decision-making. It helps organizations identify emerging market trends and customer preferences, allowing them to adapt their product offerings and marketing strategies accordingly. By staying ahead of the competition and catering to evolving customer demands, businesses can gain a competitive edge and increase market share.

Moreover, demand forecasting aids decision-making in areas such as pricing, promotions, and new product development. By understanding demand fluctuations, companies can optimize pricing strategies to maximize profitability. They can also plan targeted promotions and launch new products at the right time, increasing their chances of success in the market.

In conclusion, demand forecasting is a crucial element in decision-making for organizations operating in the realms of operations and supply chain management. Its importance lies in its ability to provide insights into future demand patterns, enabling businesses to optimize their resources, plan for capacity expansion, manage inventory effectively, and make informed strategic decisions. By harnessing the power of demand forecasting, companies can improve operational efficiency, increase customer satisfaction, and drive overall business success.

Continuous Learning and Adaptation in Demand Forecasting

In the ever-changing landscape of business, staying ahead of the competition requires organizations to be agile and responsive to market demands. This is particularly true in the realm of operations and supply chain management, where accurate demand forecasting is crucial for optimizing production, reducing costs, and satisfying customer needs. In this subchapter, we delve into the concept of continuous learning and adaptation in demand forecasting, exploring how it can enhance the effectiveness of forecasting methodologies and drive business success.

Demand forecasting is an intricate process that involves analyzing historical data, market trends, and various external factors to predict future demand for products or services. However, relying solely on historical data can be limiting, as it fails to account for the dynamic nature of markets. This is where continuous learning and adaptation come into play.

Continuous learning in demand forecasting centers around the concept of updating and refining forecasting models on an ongoing basis. By regularly incorporating new data and insights, organizations can enhance the accuracy of their forecasts and make more informed decisions. This process involves analyzing internal data, such as sales figures, customer feedback, and production metrics, as well as external data sources like market research reports, industry trends, and economic indicators. By collecting and analyzing a broad range of data, businesses can gain a comprehensive understanding of market dynamics and adjust their forecasts accordingly.

Adaptation, on the other hand, refers to the ability to modify forecasting strategies based on changing circumstances. This requires a flexible approach to demand forecasting, where organizations are open to experimenting with different methodologies and models. By monitoring forecast accuracy and comparing it to actual demand, businesses can identify areas for improvement and adapt their forecasting techniques accordingly. This may involve incorporating advanced analytics techniques, such as machine learning and artificial intelligence, to uncover patterns and insights that traditional forecasting methods may overlook.

The benefits of continuous learning and adaptation in demand forecasting are manifold. Not only does it lead to more accurate forecasts, but it also enables businesses to respond swiftly to market fluctuations, optimize inventory management, and allocate resources effectively. Moreover, it fosters a culture of innovation and continuous improvement within the organization, as employees are encouraged to challenge traditional assumptions and explore new possibilities.

In conclusion, continuous learning and adaptation are essential components of effective demand forecasting in the field of operations and supply chain management. By embracing these principles, organizations can stay in tune with market dynamics, make better-informed decisions, and gain a competitive edge in today's rapidly evolving business landscape.